MW01248316

The Brilliant Service Professional

Building Trust, Creating Value, Having Fun

Praise for *The Brilliant Service Professional*

"*The Brilliant Service Professional* is a fantastic road map to success. Whether a seasoned executive or just cutting your professional teeth, the Brilliant Practices and Shining Examples reinforce our foundation and motivate us to be the best. Alex Alexander is Tom Hopkins, Harvey Mackay, and Malcolm Gladwell all wrapped into one. In our new service economy, *BSP* will help advance our position in the world market. If you have customers, you need to read this book!"

Chris Zane
Founder and President
Zane's Cycles, and
Author of Reinventing the Wheel:
The Science of Creating Lifetime Customers

"Alexander has a knack for taking mind-bending and snore-worthy topics and turning them into a magnetic read. Readers of *The Brilliant Service Professional* who take his advice will become service pro rock stars. They'll boost their relationships, build a dynamite personal brand, gain job security, roll in the dough, and have a blast doing it all."

Meryl K. Evans
Senior Editor
InternetViZ

"A fine book that is inspiring, yet also effectively grounded in the needed competencies, tools, and behaviors to be an extraordinary service professional."

Stephen W. Brown, PhD
Founder and Distinguished Faculty
Center for Services Leadership
W. P. Carey School of Business
Arizona State University and
Strategic Partner, The INSIGHT Group

"Alex Alexander does it again! *The Brilliant Service Professional* is the definitive step-by-step guide to creating rock-star service performance—one that allows you to dominate the competition through world-class service. It is a must-read for any serious service professional. I highly recommend it."

David Rippe
President
Celestia International

"*The Brilliant Service Professional* focuses on the single greatest asset a company has—its people. The book provides strategies to help service professionals become corporate rock stars and provides insights for them, and their organizations, to capture their full potential."

Darin Chartier
Director of Customer Services
Agie Charmilles

"I have known Dr. Alexander for many years, and have always enthusiastically waited for his next publication. In this new effort, Alex zeroes in on the individuals sitting in the vital role of delivering service within the organization. He equates the service professional to a rock star and reveals the attributes that enable brilliant performance. This is a concise and fast read and challenges all of us to travel the road to brilliance. I highly recommend it."

Walt Gasparovic
Chairman and CEO
The Society for Service Executives

The Brilliant Service Professional

Building Trust, Creating Value, Having Fun

James "Alex" Alexander

Alexander Consulting

The Brilliant Service Professional:
Building Trust, Creating Value, Having Fun

© 2013 James A. Alexander

This edition published by Alexander Consulting, Fort Myers, FL.

First Edition

ISBN 978-0-9832260-1-7

In Memoriam
To Hank Stroll, a brilliant service professional.

Table of Contents

The Brilliant Service Professional

The New Corporate Rock Star

Rock stars are the brand of the band, the go of the show, and the keys to the fees. They muster the luster and provide the honey that lures the money.

In Corporate Earth, the service professional is claiming center stage.

I know what you're thinking: A service person as a rock star?

Let me answer your question by asking a question. Do you know any executives who are not interested in providing a marvelous customer experience, building deep, trust-based relationships with key customers, expanding business in existing accounts, getting new customers easier and faster, and dominating the competition?

Senior managers from all types of businesses in all types of industries are discovering that one role takes the spotlight in deepening key relationships with key accounts. Whatever title individuals in that position are given—field service technician, support engineer, implementation consultant, services account manager, resident engineer, technical account manager—no one has more potential impact on the success of the company and its key customers than the service professional...no one. High-performing service pros are where the action is, orchestrating a superb customer experience, proactively preventing problems before they occur, and leveraging relationships to rock out customers and lock out the competition.[1]

Research Validation: What Execs Say

Following are some executive comments taken from my research[2] that reveal the power of the rock-star service professional.

One senior executive from a huge telecommunications company talked about it in terms of competitive advantage:

"Our lifeblood depends on the capabilities of our top service personnel to differentiate our company from others in the industry. They understand our customers' issues and are creative in developing solutions to address them. They have become evangelists for our products and solutions and are often used in pre-sales situations to demonstrate our capabilities."

A manager from a European software company talked about finding new opportunities:

"Frequently, the customer doesn't know that we can help him with some other problem he is dealing with. Our top technical service people recognize and capitalize on these opportunities and we both win—the customer wins by having their needs served better, and we win by building our business and achieving revenue goals."

A global head of services for a manufacturing company put it this way:

"Our field engineers make one million customer calls per year. When they build deep relationships, our customer loyalty soars. We must maximize this opportunity."

Obviously this is a topic of significance to business leaders and an evolution/revolution worth pursuing!

Flash Point: Unleash your service brilliance!

The Attributes of the Brilliant Service Professional

OK, so you're convinced. But you're probably wondering: What does a brilliant service professional (BSP) look like?

Brilliant service professionals are, well, brilliant, and their glow lights the way to stellar performance.

The figure below illustrates the attributes of the BSP. Let's review this diagram from right to left, starting with the results: repeatable, sustainable performance.

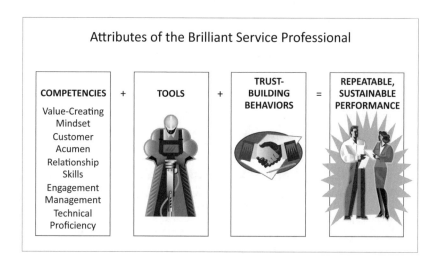

Attributes of the Brilliant Service Professional

COMPETENCIES	+	TOOLS	+	TRUST-BUILDING BEHAVIORS	=	REPEATABLE, SUSTAINABLE PERFORMANCE
Value-Creating Mindset Customer Acumen Relationship Skills Engagement Management Technical Proficiency						

Repeatable, Sustainable Performance

When service professionals rock, the outputs are repeatable, sustainable, value-adding performance. The impact is huge: Loyal customers get phenomenal value from their investment in your company and sing your praises far and wide. Your company achieves strong, profitable growth, in both products and services, and locks out the competition. And you, the brilliant service pro, get the rewards and recognition befitting your contribution and your status. Sounds like a classic win-win-win to me!

Trust-Building Behaviors

Brilliant service professionals get brilliant results by behaving differently from average service providers. They must do many things well, as you'll see in Chapter 1, but rock-star service pros act in ways that quickly build and maintain integrity. BSPs ooze credibility as they actively apply the seven builders of trust that we'll discuss in Chapter 2.

Tools

The service rock star is a big believer in using tools. He enthusiastically embraces any checklist of required actions, set of practices, or relevant case study that can help him retain quality while doing his job faster and easier. You will find examples of tools used by BSPs throughout the book, particularly in Chapter 7.

Competencies

Five competencies are integrated within the brilliant service professional:

1. **Value-creating mindset.** The brilliant service professional possesses a view of life based on creating value. He understands the big picture and collaborates with customers and colleagues to deliver business results and personal wins. Here is what executives have said on this topic:
   - "They build upon their credibility and relationship skills to find bigger customer needs and recommend appropriate solutions."
   - "They understand the big picture."

- "Our top performers have a holistic viewpoint. They clearly see the importance and the fit of services and support as part of the overall solution when combined with hardware, software, and consumables. Our average performers fail to leverage the strength and diversity of our entire organization."
- "They have a program-level horizon instead of a project-level horizon."
- "They look beyond their role with regard to 'what would the CEO want to know?'"

   Examples of this value-creating mindset will be provided throughout the book.

2. **Customer acumen.** The BSP knows a lot about his customers. He understands his customer's industry, his customer's markets, his company's competitors, and his customer's competitors. Furthermore, he is savvy about business in general. Executive comments regarding customer acumen include:
   - "They have knowledge of both the client's environment and our business. They take the trouble to understand more, and it pays off."
   - "They have a better grasp of overall business needs."
   - "They bring a rich portfolio of practical experiences and relationships with others, and they possess an understanding of business dynamics and market trends."

   Chapter 3 is devoted to exploring this important competency and explaining how to build and use it effectively.

3. **Relationship skills.** The brilliant service professional knows that relationships are what matter in work and in all aspects of life. He is a master of the four core relationship skills of listening with intensity, probing with purpose, presenting powerfully, and acknowledging concerns. Again, here are some direct quotes from my research participants that emphasize the criticality of these skills:
   - "My top performers possess not just adequate or good

communication skills, they have great communication skills."

- "They communicate the invisible well."
- "They display superior creativity in listening to customer issues and creating a solution strategy that clearly shows how it solves the problem quickly and thoroughly. The differentiator is their level of creativity, their understanding of issues, and the speed with which they react."
- "They are superb communicators with clients, team members, and management within our company."
- "They find a way to outline options and pros and cons to the customer in such a way that this becomes the customer's direction."

The four core relationship skills will be discussed in depth in Chapter 4.

4. **Engagement management.** The BSP understands how engagements are run, how problems are solved, and how to best interact with the customer. Internally, he uses the knowledge management system, follows procedures, uses prescribed tools, and provides accurate updates on all work in a timely fashion.

The five steps of engagement management relevant to every service pro are explained in Chapter 5.

5. **Technical proficiency.** The brilliant service pro knows enough about his technology, products, and services to get things done. Interestingly, deep technical know-how is not vital in most situations. Here are some comments from my research that demonstrate this point:

- "My star performers are all good technically, however, most are not technical experts — they know when to bring in technical gurus when needed."
- "Interestingly, many of my people who customers see as trusted advisors are only technically adequate. They deliver their value through helping customers connect

the dots—showing how the best use of our solutions can have a big impact on that customer's issues."

My assumption is that you are already technically competent, and therefore I will focus my writing on the other attributes that make up the rock-star service professional.

So there you have it: Five competencies that are enhanced by tools and mobilized by trust-building behaviors that will yield the results that customers crave and executives yearn for.

The Goal of This Book

Whether you are just starting out in service or are an experienced pro, my goal is the same: build upon your existing talents and experience to achieve the distinguished level of being seen by your customers, your peers, your boss, and your company as a high-value contributor to success—a brilliant service professional. Like anything of value, it will take some work, but the good news is that the attributes are known, the skills determined, and the steps to success defined. Follow my advice and you will succeed. It is as simple as that.

What's in It for You?
If you apply the knowledge within the covers of this book and become a brilliant service professional, you will:

- **Provide greater customer impact.** A brilliant service professional takes charge of the customer experience and makes recommendations that drive the most value. They get personal fulfillment out of providing great impact.
- **Create great relationships.** Customers highly value people who improve their business and personal situation, and thus appreciate having a relationship with a brilliant service professional. They also are willing to become reference accounts

for the service professional's company, which makes getting more customers both easier and faster.

- **Achieve recognition.** An advantage of being in a customer-facing role is that top performers get lots of recognition because of the visibility they achieve and the huge value they bring to customers and to their employers. Who doesn't like to be well known and respected?

- **Build your personal brand.** The word gets out when you are the very best. As a top performer, you'll build your brand throughout your company and the industry in which you work.

- **Enjoy job security.** The very best performers in any profession in any industry are never without a job, whatever the state of the economy. If you are a BSP, the worst thing that will happen in a downturn is that you will land a position with greater opportunities!

- **Make more money.** Brilliant service professionals are in short supply, and the best ones make very good money. You can be financially secure and enjoy the lifestyle you want.

- **Have more fun.** Brilliant service professionals take pride in their roles, their accomplishments, and their relationships. They do important work that makes a difference. Isn't that what fun is all about?

Becoming a brilliant service pro can be a life-changer for many individuals. In this book, you will learn the knowledge, skills, and mindset required to be the rock star of your organization. Within months of dedicating yourself to becoming a BSP, you'll hear the roar of the crowd!

What You Will Learn
You will learn the multiple potential benefits of effectively behaving as a brilliant service professional. You will discover what differentiates the rock stars of service from everyone else. You

will discover the research-based and field-proven core and best (brilliant) practices, lessons learned, and benchmarks for success.

In addition, you'll learn what doesn't work, the common worst practices that hamper and sometimes kill services attempts, and how to effectively avoid them, or at least lessen their impact. Also, I'll share examples and make recommendations that, if implemented as suggested, will both speed and smooth your transition to becoming a brilliant service professional.

Here are some of the key themes and core content that are explored and explained in this book:

- Executives' changing expectations of the service provider.
- The trust-building behaviors that differentiate the brilliant service pro from everyone else.
- The four core relationship skills that must be mastered for outstanding communication.
- How the BSP influences with integrity to help the customer become more successful.
- Potholes on the path to perfect performance.
- The requirements necessary to deliver on the customer promise.
- Why under-promise and over-deliver is a bad idea.
- What BSPs do that others don't do.
- How to establish trust fast, using the seven trust-building behaviors.
- How to build your customer acumen to communicate in the way the customer wants.
- How to build confidence and create urgency in getting the customer to do the right thing.
- Understanding the three types of customers and how to handle each one.
- How to plan for and engage customers in worthwhile conversations.
- How executives differ and how best to communicate with them.

- Understanding how to create value.
- How to create relentless repeatability.
- The BSP's role in building loyalty and creating customer champions.
- Effectively working with sales and other departments.
- A qualifying process that is both effective and efficient.
- The service pro's role in helping to get new business.
- How to say no with confidence and style.
- Building your personal brand.
- Avoiding scope creep.
- Mastering your work-life balance.
- Planning and preparing for peak personal performance.
- Personal leadership—how to take charge of your job and have fun.
- Scores of brilliant practices that you can implement immediately.
- Other good stuff.

Who Should Read This Book?
This book is designed for *anyone in business who touches the customer*, especially:

- **Business-to-business (B2B) service providers.** From the field service technician fixing equipment, to the customer support engineer dealing with tough software problems over the phone, to the technology consultant advising executives in the boardroom—all B2B service providers will see immediate relevance.
- **Business-to-consumer (B2C) service providers.** From the phone company response center associate directing calls, to the local cable installer connecting residences, to the financial stockbroker vying for new business—all B2C service providers will gain quickly by applying the concepts found in this book.

If the success of your career is directly related to your ability to effectively work with customers, you will benefit from this book.

Others who will benefit from reading this book include:

- Professionals dealing with "inside" customers.
- Service managers tasked with improving service performance.
- Technical managers trying to increase the "soft skills" of their technical talent.
- Sales managers trying to sell more products, easier and faster.
- Executives looking for ways to create customer loyalty and build competitive advantage.
- Internal practitioners (e.g., human resources, training, organization development, quality) desiring to do a better job with their internal customers.
- External practitioners (e.g., analysts, management consultants) attempting to do a better job with their clients.
- Nonprofit service providers. (Although the organization goals and context are different, the required service provider mindset and capabilities are the same. You will just need to tolerate the business jargon and translate the concepts to your situation.)
- People tired of boring theoretical business books who are looking for something practical and more enjoyable to read that will take their performance to new levels.

What's the Basis of This Book?

This book is research-based, field-proven, and focused on the vital few requirements necessary for the success of the service professional. I'll share with you what I've learned during more than two decades of personally marketing, selling, and performing services; observing, training, and coaching services professionals; and advising, consulting, and counseling services leaders.

This book is easy to understand, simple to execute, and you'll see immediate results from applying what you learn. Each chapter provides information critical to the service professional, explained in an easy-to-grasp way with examples for how to apply it.

Full Disclosure
Over a lifetime of involvement with a variety of organizations — large and small, huge and tiny — I have worked with executives, managers, and professionals in all sorts of roles: consultants, sellers, marketers, researchers, operations specialists, and more. However, it is the service folks that I like and admire most. This group is highly talented, dedicated, soft-spoken, and as nonpolitical as the laws of organization survival will tolerate. I am extremely pleased to see and support their expanding responsibilities and witness them gain the recognition they so greatly deserve. So if you sense some pro-service bias, it's because that's how I feel.

Further Clarification
Throughout the book you'll find three types of call-outs designed to improve readability:
- **Flash Point.** These are important concepts worth pondering.
- **Brilliant Practice.** A distinguishing action deserving of a standing ovation or curtain call.
- **Shining Example.** The specific and proven application of a Brilliant Practice.

A Final Word to the Reader

This book addresses an important topic that deserves serious attention. In fact, I've devoted many years of my life to learning the ins and outs of service success. However, I've attempted to add a dash of humor and the occasional tongue-in-cheek comment to make the writing process more fun for me and the reading process more enjoyable for you. Your tolerance is appreciated if my attempts at jocularity miss their intended mark!

Don't wait for the fat lady to sing. Grab the microphone and head for the spotlight—center stage is awaiting its service star.

Rock on!

CHAPTER 1

The Transformation

From Traditional Service Provider to Brilliant Service Professional

In this chapter, I start by describing the hefty expectations and requirements of the traditional service provider. Next, I outline all the challenges, or "potholes," that get in the way of delivering on the service promise. Then, I explain the changing expectations that service executives have regarding their top service people. From there, I share the secret sauce—what brilliant service professionals do that others don't do, translated into the new requirements of those wishing to achieve brilliant service professional (BSP) status.

The Traditional Business Model

In the traditional business model, service providers are not brought into the customer mix until after the customer has made a purchase. What customers hope they have purchased is not a bundle of hardware or a list of services to be performed, but a promise—a promise that will solve a problem or improve business performance or minimize hassle or make his or her personal life easier or better. Except for the techies in the buying organization, no one really cares about RAM or ROM, milliseconds or terabytes, resolution or constitution; all they want are business results and personal wins. That's it.

Once the customer has made the purchase, it is the role of the services organization and the service provider to deliver on that promise. If that goes well, then the service provider has added a big dose of value and has helped turn the customer into a client—an account that buys from your company again and again.

Flash Point: Customers are good; clients are better.

Figure 1.1 shows the six requirements of the traditional service provider. The first three requirements revolve around deliver-

Figure 1.1

Requirements of the Traditional Service Provider

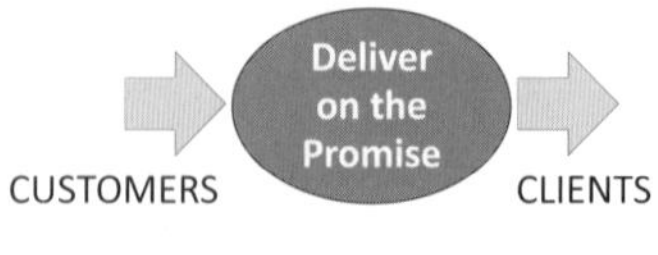

CUSTOMERS → Deliver on the Promise → CLIENTS

Deliver on the promise consistently:
- Do service work on time, within budget, and up to defined quality standards.
- Communicate appropriately with the customer when needed.
- Respond enthusiastically when asked about your organization's capabilities.

Meet internal expectations:
- Use knowledge management system, follow procedures, and utilize tools as prescribed.
- Provide accurate updates on all work in a timely fashion.
- Follow HR practices and be a good company citizen.

ing on the promise and are external expectations, while the other three requirements outline steps to meeting internal expectations.

Customer Expectations: Delivering on the Promise
Meeting Time, Budget, and Quality Commitments

In order to deliver on the promise, the major expectation of both the customer and the supplier is that the service provider will do the service work on time, within budget, and up to defined quality standards. When the right resources are deployed in the right way at the right place at the right time, things sing, the customer applauds, and all is good with the world.

Of course "service work" varies tremendously from job to job, from market to market, from industry to industry, and often from customer to customer. I classify services into three main buckets, as seen in Figure 1.2. You and your services team may be involved in one, two, or all three types of services.

Figure 1.2

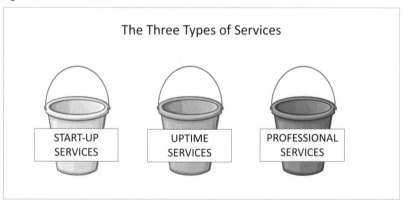

The Three Types of Services

START-UP SERVICES

UPTIME SERVICES

PROFESSIONAL SERVICES

- **Start-up services.** You may be involved in getting the product up and running by installing hardware, implementing software, or commissioning an entire plant. Depending on the situation, you may be doing the work yourself, leading third-party service pros, or training the customer on proper usage and maintenance. You could be physically at the customer's location with your sleeves rolled up and sweat on your brow, or you might be sipping on a latté and munching on a garlic bagel while guiding the customer through start-up procedures over the phone.

- **Uptime services.** Many service providers are heavily focused on delivering uptime services. Once the hardware, software, or whatever-ware is operational after start-up, the service job of keeping things up and running is foremost. Fix it fast when it breaks, or better yet, prevent it from breaking through means of ongoing monitoring, preemptive consultation, and preventive maintenance. Those involved in uptime services are the many support professionals who spend their day solving customers' product functionality problems over the phone, the tens of thousands of field service engineers (FSEs) who are dispatched to customer locations hourly and get broken products up and running, and the service account managers (SAMs) who are brought in to expedite an escalation for a down network.
- **Professional services.** Some service jobs may entail going "beyond the box" to impact customers' processes and systems through the delivery of professional services. Whatever the title, when delivering professional services, this service provider is in the role of technology consultant, spending his time conducting audits, performing assessments, certifying customer personnel, streamlining processes, or training customer technicians in an effort to improve the customer's business performance.

Sometimes the time, cost, or quality performance standard of delivering on the customer promise is relatively easy to meet. All it takes is having the right resources and doing the right things the right way at the right time in the right place. A combination of robust, easy-to-use products, seamless processes, proven, intuitive tools, and smart, open-minded customers can make servicing a breeze for the capable service provider. Simple and straightforward, eh? One would think so, but we will talk about what can go wrong shortly.

Communicate Appropriately

Requirement 1 is all about installing, implementing, analyzing, preventing, fixing, optimizing, integrating, and expanding. The second expectation when delivering on the promise is to communicate appropriately with the customer as needed. This is all about answering your customer's questions, explaining actions taken, discussing options, and addressing concerns, whether done in person, over the phone, via e-mail, or by chat.

Your company probably has established guidelines regarding communicating with the customer. Customer contact representatives have a script to follow. Support center personnel are provided with a knowlegebase of frequently asked questions (FAQs) to guide their customer responses and are given technical tools that make viewing customer history and product information just a click or two away.

Savvy field services organizations follow a "fix the customer first" philosophy, which requires that every contact with the customer starts with the field service engineer (FSE) confirming issues and explaining planned procedures. Once the work is complete, the FSE then reports back to the customer regarding what was done to fix the problem, along with other insights and suggestions he may have. Script outlines are developed and training is provided to get the FSE comfortable in this important communication. Tips and tools for effective communication in a variety of situations are the meat in the stew of the remainder of this book.

Respond Enthusiastically

If you do a good job of delivering on the promise by capable implementation of the first two requirements, you will have established professional credibility. When that occurs, customers will seek your advice—asking you about your company's capabilities, your thoughts on new products, or whether you feel they should change, upgrade, migrate, or whatever. When this occurs, the competent service professional responds positively and enthusiastically to these inquiries and puts the customer in contact with sales or the appropriate person.

Internal Expectations
Utilize Tools, Provide Updates, Follow Rules
As with every job, there are several requirements of the service provider inside the company. These internal expectations are not always fun and seldom exciting, but they are requirements to be met nonetheless. For the traditional service provider, they consist of the following:

- Use your company's internal knowledge management system (KMS), follow procedures, and utilize tools as prescribed.
- Provide accurate updates to both the customer and your company on all work completed or in progress in a timely fashion.
- Follow your company's human resources guidelines and be a good company citizen.

Potholes on the Path to Perfect Performance

Just like putting on an improvisation skit at a comedy club, the requirements outlined above on delivering on the promise are remarkably easy to explain but remarkably challenging to consistently perform well. As I hinted earlier and as every service provider knows, there are lots of things that can make meeting these performance expectations a challenge. Let's bring reality back into the picture and discuss some of the possible potholes on the path to perfect performance.

Pothole: Invisibility

Yes, the customer can observe you punch a keyboard or turn a wrench; however, the services you provide are primarily invisible, making it difficult for the customer to understand and evaluate success. The intangibility of service touches every aspect of delivering on the promise. We will talk later about the critical competency of how to make the intangible tangible when talking with customers about services.

Pothole: On Stage

Services are often delivered live, in real time, many times at the customer's location. Believe me, when a customer has a line down costing his company $10,000 a minute, the service provider is "on stage" as she pulls up data on a terminal on the customer's factory floor. There could well be a dozen sets of eyeballs observing her every keystroke, closely watching her face for signs that might indicate success or failure. The service provider might sense the heightened breath of the customer, feel the pressure on the back of her neck, and taste the tension in the air. At the same time, questions are probably rolling through the customer's mind like clouds during a thunderstorm: *Who is she calling on her cell phone, and why? Doesn't she know what to do? How bad is it? Is she sweating? Oh, my gosh! The Big Boss is not going to like this…there goes my bonus. Is my resume up to date? I knew I should be using LinkedIn more.*

Or consider a professional services consultant working on site on a mega enterprise resource planning (ERP) software implementation who is asked to "fill in" at the last minute for the ill project manager and is tasked with giving the monthly update to the customer's senior management team. Imagine in this setting that the first words out of the Big Boss's tightly drawn lips are, "We were discussing whether our legal counsel should be present to discuss your breach of contract. We want to know why the project is already four months late and three million euros over budget." Oh, boy! Time to suck it up and practice those relationship skills you read about. Is this high stress, or what?

Flash Point: Being a service pro is not for the faint of heart.

Pothole: Personalization

In the world of products, the goal is uniformity. Variation is controlled in the hope that all models of all products work in the same way all of the time. The goal of performing services is more complicated. Although the process of delivering the service (such as on-site equipment repair or over-the-phone problem analysis or systems integration) may be the same (and usually should be the same), the successful service provider must tailor the experience for each customer. To put it in manufacturing parlance, the service provider is dealing with "a lot size of one." For the customer to feel the personalization, the service provider must make adjustments in real time. The importance of this becomes clearer when considering the next pothole.

Pothole: Differing Expectations

Although a service provider for a computer reseller may perform exactly the same service exactly the same way for two similar businesses in the same market and in the same geography, each customer will define the quality of the service performance differently. When asked, Customer A may be thrilled with the service provider's performance, whereas Customer B may be lackluster in her feelings.

These differences in expectations may derive from the customer's personality or the customer's state of mind at the time. However, much of it comes from the customer's past experience with you, other service providers in your company, competitors of your company, or service providers providing other services. For example, Customer A may have had lousy experiences with past service providers, and thus was elated by your high-quality performance. Enjoy the adoration! Whereas Customer B may have been spoiled by routinely receiving stellar service from other providers. Live with it. Good or bad, these past experiences have set the expectation bar, and all your future performances will be measured against them.

The benefit of an experienced customer, however, is that he usually has a good idea of "how things go" and, in general, knows what realistic expectations are. Conversely, customer inexperience confounds and compounds the issue of realistic expectations. For example, a new manager coming from another part of the business who has just learned to spell "services" last week may be clueless as to what poor or OK or good service looks like. The only services performance he can relate to may be totally inappropriate. Hence, his expectations may be all over the board with regard to appropriateness and doability. Making it worse, as the inexperienced customer becomes educated about your services and the services of others, his expectations often change, adding more complexity and apprehension into the mix.

Another contributor to the differing expectation challenge is when, for whatever reason, those in the selling process did not communicate one hundred percent accurate information to the customer. Hence, customer expectations may be out of line with reality. If the information was correct but it was communicated poorly, or if the correct information was communicated accurately but the customer interpreted it differently than the intent, the customer may expect more than what is possible or different than what can be achieved.

Service documents such as service level agreements, statements of work, or letters of engagement are intended to clean up muddy water by clearly outlining the who-what-where-when-how of the agreed-upon services to be performed and the responsibilities of both customer and supplier. Care coupled with collaboration is called for in developing practical agreements.

However, no matter how masterfully crafted, you can be certain that some customers: (a) will not read the service document, (b) will read the document but not understand what it really means, or (c) will understand what is stated but interpret the meaning differently than your company intended.

All three of these scenarios are bad. Does the customer ever expect to get less quality? To receive slower response? To pay more? Never! You can be sure that in all three of these situations, if there are any differences in expectations, the customer will expect more or better or cheaper or faster than your company intended to deliver. That is why managing expectations is such an important skill set, and one we'll talk more about later.

Pothole: Wrong Product
The solution sold may not be an ideal fit for the customer's needs as is (e.g., not enough capacity, wrong configuration, inability to scale) and will require special customization (e.g., duct tape and baling wire combined with big doses of inspiration, perspiration, and frustration) to make it function. For example, the customer may have bought the wrong product because of the wrong expectations stated earlier. Or he may have bought the cheaper, lower-performing product over the recommendations of the seller, knowing it was not ideal, because it was all he could afford or because he "hoped" your company could magically make it work anyway if he begged or screamed or threatened.

Even worse, the solution may not work at all.

Pothole: Quirky Products
I'm sure you've seen it from time to time: the million-dollar piece of equipment that can't seem to stay in calibration, the enterprise software that randomly—without reason or warning—shuts down key customer processes, or the $1,000 stamper in a billion-dollar assembly line whose service cabinet takes 40 minutes to

open just for routine monthly maintenance. Since no one from engineering or product development is on the phone or in the plant when the customer shakes his head in bewilderment or snarls into the mouthpiece of the telephone, you deal with it. Guilt by association!

Pothole: Wrong Resources
There may be situations when you are not the right service provider for the issue. Not a big deal if a seamless phone transfer can remedy things. It is a big deal, though, if the customer is located in Homer, Alaska, and has already waited two days to get his mission-critical production line up and running during halibut canning season, and you show up with either the wrong expertise, the wrong testing equipment, or the wrong part. You better hope the floatplane pilot takes MasterCard.

Pothole: Customer Screw-Up
I know this would rarely happen (wink), but it is possible that the customer tinkered with the product, and tinkered poorly. The outcome is that he made a mess that now must be cleaned up. Even worse, he may not admit it; he may blame you and expect you to fix it fast…and for free.

Pothole: Bad Timing
I'll bet you can relate to these consequences of bad timing:
- The software hiccupped the day before your customer's government certification audit, putting their accreditation in jeopardy and potentially incurring huge fines for their company. Now your time-to-resolution has shifted from a normal three days to three hours.
- The equipment at your best account broke on the morning that a key sales prospect was to tour your customer's plant, and your company's sales guy is stalling over a long lunch while you sweat and toil.

- Your customer demanded that his software update be performed at midnight on Christmas Eve, and your company's salesperson committed to the customer that you would be there to do it. Nevermind that it is your tenth anniversary and you had booked a Mediterranean cruise. You are sitting in the lounge on the ship's promenade level at 11 p.m. sipping on a red-and-yellow cocktail with an umbrella in it and wondering if you will be flogged or fired when sales finds out you didn't show up for the update.

Pothole: Mother Nature
Sometimes Mother Nature gets angry and creates snowstorms, floods, hurricanes, earthquakes, volcanoes, tornadoes, tsunamis, cold waves, heat waves, and other wild weather—all seemingly in an attempt to sabotage your service work! All or any of the above conditions can cause brown-outs, black-outs, or white-outs, close airports and seaports, block freeways, or shut down subways, preventing you from delivering on the promise. Sometimes the customer understands...sometimes he doesn't.

Pothole: Dark Karma
Even with the best of planning, dark karma can take its toll. See if you can relate to any of these situations:
- You are physically exhausted from being up for the past three nights nursing two sick babies, and your mind goes totally blank in a customer meeting when you are asked a very simple question. You simply cannot function. You mumble an apology and leave the room while trying to remember if that cot in the storage room is still there and who has the key.
- Filling in for a sick colleague, you are dispatched to fix a product you know nothing about. Ziggy, the product specialist, has told you, "No worries." He has promised to talk you through the procedure over the phone. After assuring the anxious customer that all will be well soon, you dial Ziggy's

personal number on your smartphone. You hear a stressed voice message stating that Ziggy is on his way to emergency dental surgery and will be out of commission for the next two days. You ask for directions to the restroom and look around for an escape path.

- While on your way to your customer's site, you realize with horror that his office is located in a neighborhood that even RoboCop would be afraid to patrol. Not knowing what to do and fearing for your life, you keep driving until you find yourself at the Mexican border. Here your van is waved over and searched by grim-looking men dressed in khaki green with automatic weapons (you hope that they really are the Federales). While you watch them tear out your backseat, you try to conjure up your meager Spanish: "Lo siento, señor. No entiendo nada."

- You forgot your clearance badge, and the Department of Defense security not only won't let you into the computer center, but they have confiscated your briefcase and your phone and have locked you in a small glass room while they do a background check. As you thumb through the December 1988 issue of *Reader's Digest*, you are struck by déjà vu — the room reminds you exactly of the emigration detention room in which you were once held at the Kazakhstan airport; that trip did not turn out well.

- Yesterday, in a fit of anger, the new vice president fired all six engineers from product support. Being really technically strong and a good team player, you and one other colleague volunteered to man the support phones. You feel good about it because out of the company's eight product lines, you are very knowledgeable about four of them, and competent in three. You are only weak in the old Alogen line, but no customers still use it...do they?

The first four calls you pick up are about Alogen problems, and one is severe. Your colleague knows nothing either, and you can't find anything in your online knowledge man-agement system. Putting your ranting customer on hold, you grab a bottle of Tylenol as you head down the stairway to the basement hoping to find some hardcopy documents that can help fix the problem.

- You are in your home office awaiting an important confer-ence call when you hear the dishwasher running. Proud of your four-year-old son for proactively cleaning up, you go to praise the young man. Looking through the glass win-dow of the dishwasher, utter horror grasps your throat as you discover your company iPad is now in the rinse cycle. Of course, the only place the critical information you need for the impending call is on that very clean, very shiny iPad.

So there you have it. Delivering on the customer promise is not easy, and the types of obstacles that can get in your way are as varied as vacationers at Disney World. The organizations and the service providers within them that consistently do service well are adding lots and lots of value to their customers and to their companies. Kudos to those of you who make this happen. Note that if your job looks like the traditional service provider that I've described above, then most everything I discuss in this book will help you function at your most effective. However, for many of you reading this manual of self-improvement, the ser-vice game has changed, is changing, or will be changing soon, and performing the traditional role of the service provider is no longer enough. Let me tell you why.

Service Executives' Changing Expectations

Service executives in most businesses, in most markets, in most industries, in most geographies, are being asked by their bosses to do more to improve customer satisfaction, increase customer loyalty, become more efficient, help sell more product, and help sell more profitable services, often with no additional resources (and sometimes with less). The service executives I have studied have one thing in common: Each one was depending heavily upon their top service personnel to help them change their business and meet their ever-challenging goals. Every executive recognized that to be successful, their service providers would have to change their mindset, improve their skills, and increase their knowledge—in other words, assume the role of the brilliant service professional. Here are a few reflective comments from my research:

- From a professional services executive: "For my organization to be relevant and to gain the funding we need in order to grow, we have to become a strategic asset. It is up to our top service people to show that prospects buy from us because of the value they bring."
- From a director of field service: "The more I can get my service technicians to build relationships and look for new sales opportunities, the more successful we will be."
- From a CEO: "I take this transformation personally. My ability to transform those in my service organization from being reactive to being thought leaders and specialization-based will make or break my career. I am passionate about this subject."

Figure 1.3 illustrates the new expectations that service executives are looking for in their service personnel.

Figure 1.3

Changing Expectations of Service Providers: More...

Communicate Value	Trusted Advisor Role
Client Involvement	Internal Contribution
Drive Revenue	Responsibility for
Business Savvy	Personal Development

Source: Alexander, James A. 2007. *Turning Technical Experts into Trusted Advisors*. Alexander Consulting.

Communicate Value

The service execs from my research knew their people were add-ing a lot of value, but felt that often customers didn't know it. They felt that making sure that customers saw the benefit from the service provided was a big deal, and they wanted their ser-vice people to do a better job of communicating it.

Customer Involvement

Another truism from the execs was that the more their best ser-vice people interacted with customers, the better the overall re-lationship. Along with working with the customer's techies and managers, the service execs wanted their best service people to get more involved with the customer's executives.

Drive Revenue

When all of the above occurred, the natural outcome was more revenue to the company. Not only were more services bought, but more products were purchased as well. The executives wanted their top people to be more proactive in looking for opportunities, passing them on to sales or the appropriate person, or making the sale themselves.

Business Savvy

These execs new that the top people from all of their customer functions were being included in decisions involving services that affected the entire business. They observed that their service pros who were able to talk "business speak" were more effective in getting customers to do what was best for them. Connecting the dots from technology to products to business results was a differentiator — when the service professionals could relate to the customer in business terms, they were much more effective.

Trusted Advisor Role

Furthermore, executives observed that when their people had a higher level of customer involvement, were adept at communicating value, and had the ability to link benefits to the customer business, customers viewed them as trusted advisors. The executives wanted more of this deep credibility in their service professionals, as it speeded decisions and broadened opportunities.

Internal Contribution

These execs also realized that their best people could help advance the service agenda inside the company. They felt it was important that they spend more face time with their own executives, work more closely with sales, and help mentor high-potential team members.

Responsibility for Personal Development

Finally, although these executives concurred that management was responsible for providing training, coaching, and learning aids, what it really came down to was individuals taking charge of their own careers.

Requirements of the Brilliant Service Professional

Wow, the table stakes just went up! You will note that the service executives from my research wanted much more from their service people, but they didn't want them to do anything less! Hence, Figure 1.4 shows the same traditional requirements detailed above, plus the additional "rock star" requirements shown in boldface text. Since I talked about the base expectations earlier, I will only comment on the new expectations of the brilliant service professional.

Beyond the traditional requirements, the BSP delivers on the promise consistently and meets internal expectations by doing these additional things.

Figure 1.4

Requirements of the Brilliant Service Provider

CUSTOMERS   CLIENTS

Deliver on the promise consistently:
- Do service work on time, within budget, and up to defined quality standards.
- Communicate appropriately with the customer when needed.
- Respond enthusiastically when asked about your organization's capabilities.
- **Proactively look for ways to enhance the customer experience and increase customer success.**
- **Set and manage customer expectations.**
- **Immediately initiate "service recovery" when a customer situation goes south.**

Meet internal expectations:
- Use knowledge management system, follow procedures, and utilize tools as prescribed.
- Provide accurate updates on all work in a timely fashion.
- Follow HR practices and be a good company citizen.
- **Consult with executives and sales.**
- **Contribute insights into product development and service development.**
- **Mentor high-potential colleagues.**

Customer Expectations: Delivering on the Promise
Be Proactive

Topping the list of new requirements is to proactively look for ways to enhance the customer experience and increase customer success. This is an attitude adjustment. In the traditional service provider role, almost everything was reactive. Here the requirement is to actively look for, examine, contemplate, consider, postulate, and speculate on any and all possible ways to make things easier, better, or faster for the customer. If this is done effectively and appropriately, your customers will receive more value, and your company will be rewarded by new business.

Set and Manage Expectations

As was painfully demonstrated earlier, often customers begin their service experience with you and your service team by having the wrong expectations. The brilliant service professional takes responsibility for setting and managing appropriate customer expectations, beginning on day one. Adjusting false assumptions, explaining reality, and setting the scenario right rest squarely on the BSP's broad shoulders. Setting and managing customer expectations includes tactful explanation of what can and will be done, addressing concerns empathetically while explaining what won't be done, saying no when necessary, and always communicating the rationale for decisions.

Initiate Service Recovery

It is vital to immediately initiate service recovery when a customer situation goes south. If you deal with complex products or solutions implemented in complex sophisticated environments, occasionally things will break, and sometimes they will break badly. At times it is the customer's fault, other times it is a partner's fault, sometimes your company made a mistake, and sometimes you messed up. When a situation is serious, the BSP doesn't argue fault or pass judgment or wait for approval; the BSP initiates action.

Internal Expectations

Consult with Your Executives and Sales

The BSP has more knowledge about the customer and more customer credibility than anyone in your company. Your executives need these insights to create strategy, determine business focus, and allocate resources. Furthermore, to truly manage key accounts, sales and services must work together in creating an account plan and jointly implementing it.

Contribute Insights

Contributing your insights to product development and service development results in a win-win for your company and for your customers. BSPs use their knowledge of key customers and their strong communication skills to help product development consider product servicing from the beginning of the new product development process. When design for service (DFS) is implemented, both cost of service and ease of service are increased, thereby positively impacting business financials for the life of the product. And who is in a better position to offer ideas for new value-adding services than the BSP?

Mentor High-Potential Colleagues
Closing the gap between being talented and being effective can take months or even years for the service professional. Top services businesses ask their BSPs to help in this effort in order to shorten the developmental period. A side benefit to the BSP is that it is usually rewarding and fun.

From Traditional Service Provider to Brilliant Service Professional

Figure 1.5 simplifies, summarizes, and magnifies the changes required to transform from a traditional service provider to a brilliant service professional.[1]

Reactive + Proactive
For most service pros, much of their time is spent being reactive to issues and solving problems. These challenges must continue to be addressed both effectively and efficiently. However, the BSP seizes the initiative and aggressively looks for ways to prevent problems and find new opportunities that will benefit the customer. BSPs are not afraid to challenge existing standards and explore new ways of thinking.

Figure 1.5

From Traditional Service Provider to Brilliant Service Professional

Reactive ————————— + —— Proactive
Tactical ———————————— + —— Strategic
Control ——————————— + —— Collaborate
Value Adder ——————— + —— Value Creator
Technical Acumen ———— + —— Customer Acumen
Professional Trust ———— + —— Personal Trust
Good Communication Skills ——➤ Great Communication Skills

Source: Alexander, James A. 2007. *Turning Technical Experts into Trusted Advisors.* Alexander Consulting.

Tactical + Strategic

Will BSPs need to be in the weeds sometimes? Of course. Ideally, they are passing off much of the technical aspects of customer issues to other team members, and they must stay abreast of ongoing issues. Yet, the BSP is a big-picture thinker, focusing on the future of his accounts and how he can have the biggest impact.

Control + Collaborate

When facing time-sensitive customer issues, are there times when it is best for the BSP to take control and work with his service team to just "git 'er done?" Yes. But the BSP realizes that significant positive change requires collaboration. The BSP mindset is to put the customer first, and then align plans and actions so that the customer and the company and the BSP all win. Attempting change without participation is like trying to make bread without the yeast—it won't rise to the occasion.

Value Adder + Value Creator

Responding to issues quickly and effectively, and then communicating the benefit to the customer, adds value. However, proactively and strategically developing recommendations that are accepted by the customer creates new value. The BSP aggressively looks for these opportunities whether they are asked to or not.

Technical Acumen + Customer Acumen

Do brilliant service professionals need to have an acceptable level of technical acumen? Absolutely. But they rely on their technical team of experts as much as possible. In addition to technical acumen, however, the BSP excels in customer acumen—having a very solid knowledge of his customer's business, their industry, their marketplace, and business in general.

Professional Trust + Personal Trust

BSPs, like traditional service providers, have earned professional trust by applying their knowledge and skills to effectively and efficiently solve customer problems. BSPs go a step further, however, by earning the personal trust of their customers. This heightened level of trust helps customers to broaden their thinking, allowing them to confidently take bigger risks or move in new directions.

From Good to Great Communication Skills

The BSP's capabilities go beyond having good communication skills. They work, hone, and sharpen the four core skills reviewed in Chapter 4 that result in great communication skills. In fact, the executives in my research stated that this is the most important differentiator between their stars and everyone else.

I understand that you have a big workload and limited time. You may feel that by the time you meet the demands of your main services work, you have little (if any) time left for being proactive. Nonetheless, by applying the strategies and tactics in this book, you can act like a BSP when it is most appropriate. In fact, by practicing what I preach, I predict that you will be able to do more, better and faster. Chapter 8 will show you how.

Is this a big change? Yes! It is a lot to ask? It sure is. Is the role of the brilliant service professional right for everyone? No, it is a choice — your choice. Being very good in the traditional role is a worthy profession, however, if you want to become a BSP, you can do it!

In the next chapter we explore, in detail, the powerful concept of building and keeping trust.

CHAPTER 2

It's All About Trust

Relationships are the key to business success. If we think of a relationship as a house, then trust is the foundation; the sturdier the base, the stronger the structure.

In this chapter, I discuss the benefits of trust, the indicators of having high trust, what we know about trust, and the seven trust builders you can use to build high levels of trust quickly. I also demonstrate why "under-promise and over-deliver" is usually a bad idea. Furthermore, I share Brilliant Practices in building trust and Shining Examples that you can apply to your work.

Benefits of Trust

When your customers trust you, many benefits are bestowed upon you.[1] They treat you with respect, share information with you that they might not have otherwise shared, act on your recommendations, ask for your advice, and in difficult scenarios give you the benefit of the doubt. What follows are explanations and examples of each of these valuable benefits.

Treat You with Respect

When you are trusted, you are treated as you wish to be treated. You are not looked upon as a second-class citizen or as a lackey solely there to do the customer's bidding. Rather, you are respected as an equal, a peer, a colleague. When you are treated with respect, much of the stress of initial contact and formal communication goes away. In effect, visiting your customer feels more like stopping by to see good friends instead of visiting your prospective in-laws for the first time. At this point in your relationship, you have both personal trust and professional trust.

Customer: "Sammy, it's great to see you! Tell me how that family vacation of yours went. I told my wife about it and now she wants to go there also."

Share Information

When you have trust, the customer is much more likely to share information with you that helps you help them.

Customer: "Here is the information you requested in full. Also, I thought you might like to see an internal analysis we conducted last quarter. It might give you some insights as to our thinking. Is there anything else you need?"

Act on Your Recommendations

When you are trusted, the customer is inclined to accept and act on your recommendations. The customer believes that you have his best interests at heart, and thus will hop to it. He will not wait for a second opinion, ask for more detail, or request additional analysis.

Customer: "OK, I've bought in to your recommendation. What do we need to get going?"

Reach for Your Advice

When you have trust, the customer will reach for your advice.

Customer: "What about your latest product that your sales

guy was telling me about—is it as good as he says? Should I buy it?"

Give You the Benefit of the Doubt

This is a big one! Let me give you an example to demonstrate the importance of this benefit.

Imagine that you are the brand-new service account manager at a very difficult but very important account. Things have not gone well during the last year, and your introductory call isn't going well either. It might sound something like this:

Customer (loud, agitated voice): "So you are our new SAM? Who did you tick off in your company to get us as an account? Do you know what a screwed-up outfit you work for? We have had three, yes, three, major outages in the last seven months. Do you know how that makes me look to the big bosses? And guess what? Ten minutes ago I got a call that the situation is going south one more time. I am sick and tired of this. Forget your escalation process—I want the phone number of your president, and I want it now!"

Yikes, that is not a fun situation. Let's fast-forward six months. You have been working long and hard with this difficult account. Coordinating the work, getting stuff done right, letting them know you care, and giving them regular updates (both good and bad). It has not been easy, but you have earned the customer's trust little by little, day after day. They renewed their contract and requested keeping you as their SAM. Now you get an unexpected phone call from this customer.

Customer (loud, agitated voice): "You guys did it again! That problem we thought we fixed just came back. What is wrong with you guys? I have half a notion...(silence, then a sigh)...Oh, jeez, sorry Sammy. I let off some steam. What do we do next?"

This is the same customer, with maybe a worse technical situation, but what a world of difference in how you were treated. Escalation was averted, hassles were minimized, probably a saved account—all because of the personal trust you had built. Your past performance earned you the benefit of the doubt...and that is huge!

Indicators of High Trust

So how do you know you have achieved high levels of customer trust? What are the indicators? Here are three:

1. **Customers or prospective customers ask for you by name.**
   Customer: "OK, Mr. Salesperson. I will sign the contract on one condition—Sammy Sampson is assigned to my account."
   Customer: "If you assure me that we can have Connie lead the implementation like she did the last time, I am ready to commit."

Flash Point: Feel the force of the BSP!

2. **You have such a strong personal brand that people seek you out for speaking engagements, writing articles, or special client assignments.** When you are really good and a professional worthy of trust, you will be asked to do things beyond your job description.
   Customer: "Sammy, I have a big favor to ask. Would you come speak at our tech managers meeting next month? I think they would find your insights valuable."
3. **You can have a ponytail, wear Hawaiian shirts, make the (occasional) smart comment, and executives still love you!** When you have earned trust, you have earned the right to look and act a little differently, if you so choose.
   Customer (said with broad smile): "Sammy, when are

you going to cut that thing off! After seeing you, my boy wants to grow a ponytail."

Trust Considerations

Here are some realities about trust to keep in mind:

1. **Trust is earned, not bought.** You can't print the words "Trusted Advisor" on your business card and expect people to believe it. In fact, many people would consider it boastful, manipulative, or assuming. Trust is something customers bestow on those they feel deserve it.

   Let me share a relevant example: I had a client wanting to expand into professional services. The need was present and the possibilities looked bright. However, research with existing customers squashed the initiative. Here is a customer response that captures the importance of trust and shows why we slammed the door on the initiative: "I don't care how smart your people are! You can't even deliver decent support today. Why would I trust you with more important services?"

2. **Building trust takes time.** Think about people you trust in your personal life. How long did you know them until they gained your trust? Weeks? Months? Never? It is the same in business situations. Interestingly, although it may take years to build trust, it takes only seconds to lose it. Hence, you have to safeguard it like a miser would protect a strongbox full of pieces of eight.

3. **The amount of trust required varies according to the situation.** Think about trust in terms of yourself. If your barber or hairstylist is on vacation, you might at random pull into a hair salon close to your office and trust that a stylist will do at least a decent job. The amount of risk is low.

   If you had a mild toothache and your dentist was unavailable, you'd probably accept the word of a friend and set up an appointment with a dentist she recommends. The amount of risk is greater, but if you trust your friend, the chance of a bad outcome is probably low.

However, if your general practitioner says your blood test shows the possibility of a rare, possibly deadly disorder, the level of trust you need to take action has shot to the top. You will most likely make an appointment with the specialist your doctor recommends, but you will probably spend hours online not only researching the disease, but also the qualifications of the top specialists in this field. Even then you may want to get a second or even a third opinion before acting. It is not that you don't trust your doctor; it is that the potential risk is really big, and hence, more effort and caution are needed.

Flash Point: The more important the service is to the customer and the higher perceived risk, the greater your level of trust must be.

4. **Your role and position automatically impact customer trust.** We all make subconscious decisions based upon our past experiences that shape our initial levels of trust for different roles. For example, although there are thousands of high-integrity salespeople deserving of trust, almost everyone at some time in their life has come in contact with low-integrity, highly manipulative, blood-sucking sellers.[2] Even just one very negative encounter causes wariness regarding all salespeople. It is like an invisible "BS indicator" emerges out of the top of your head and starts to scan for signals of insincerity whenever you hear or read the words "sales," "account manager," "business development specialist," or similar terms.

Let me give you an example you may have seen: I've had the chance to observe many supplier/customer meetings over the decades, often the final big presentation trying to land the big deal. In those conference-room settings, one trust-related scene almost always plays out. At one point in the meeting, the Big Customer looks the salesperson in the eye and asks, "Can your product do XYZ?" Within three nanoseconds the salesperson says, "Yes." Before the hiss of the "s" of his yes has been heard, all eyes in the room leap from the face of the seller to the face of the service person. What are they looking for? The truth.

Even though they may have just met you, they know you are a service guy, and service guys don't make commission; they are there to do what's best for the customer. They trust you much more than the sales guy or his boss or the fellow from marketing. So they are looking for truth indicators. Are you grimacing, squirming in the chair, or staring at the floor with your hand over your forehead? Are beads of sweat forming on your brow? If so, no go. Or are you sagely nodding your head in agreement? If so, deal done. It can be as simple as that.

Flash Point: Customers trust service people more than salespeople, and more than just about any other group in your company.

5. **Trust goes both ways.** Before you get carried away and mount a full-frontal, trust-building attack on all your accounts, remember that just like the tango, it takes two to dip and dive without falling on your face. Sometimes customers see a situation as of little importance, so they don't see trust as an issue. Some customers see all suppliers as easily

replaceable vendors providing easily replaceable commodi-
ties. Your trust-building efforts with these customers will be
a waste. However, some customers want relationships and
will invest the time and money that yield mutual trust. That
is where to focus your trust-building energy. I will give you
some recommendations on deciding where to put your trust-
building efforts in Chapter 8.

The Seven Trust Builders: Compressing the Cycle Time of Trust

Seven interrelated behaviors, illustrated in Figure 2.1, interact
to help the brilliant service professional speed trust building. A
word of warning: At first blush, these seven behaviors may seem
quite basic. Explore them deeper. You will find that these powerful practices are core tenets of not only a good business professional, but they are also the building blocks of being a good
citizen of the planet.

Figure 2.1

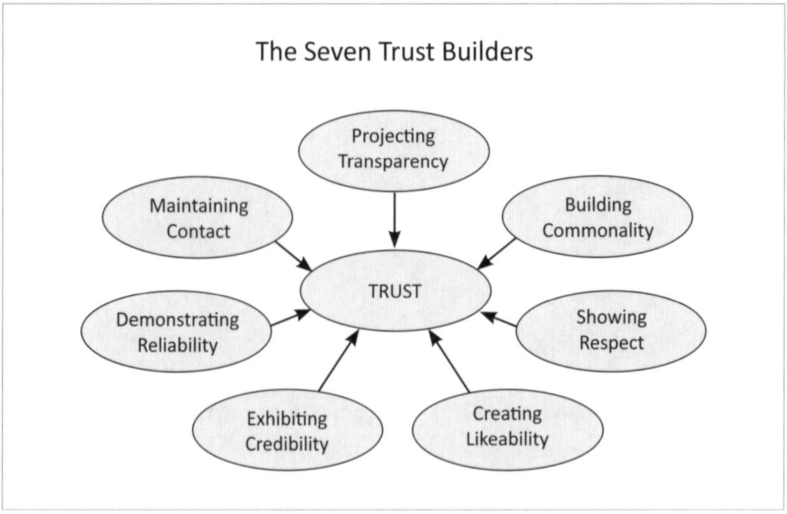

The Seven Trust Builders

- Projecting Transparency
- Maintaining Contact
- Building Commonality
- TRUST
- Demonstrating Reliability
- Showing Respect
- Exhibiting Credibility
- Creating Likeability

Trust Builder 1: Projecting Transparency

Projecting transparency involves being open and honest at all times. We all know the importance of being open and honest. We appreciate people who come across as real and who act with integrity. Being open and honest is even more important as we are confronted with growing business and societal examples of non-transparency: salespeople saying things that are not exactly correct, politicians telling half-truths, company spokespeople denying wrongdoing by their organizations, and so on. People find it refreshing (and yes, trust-building) when they know someone is being transparent, is not putting on airs, and is acting with integrity — especially when doing so is awkward or embarrassing or even painful.

Brilliant Practice: Do what you know is right. Avoid the temptation to fudge the truth or hide reality — what would your grandma think if she found out?

Here are a few Shining Examples. When offered sincerely, appropriate BSP responses such as these not only minimize potential customer irritancy, but they also build trust.

- "Ms. Customer, I'm experienced and proficient with most all issues dealing with rocket science, but I am not an expert in dealing with biophysics. However, I do know the best and the brightest person in our company who is. May I have her contact you?"

- "Mr. Customer, this is embarrassing, but I need to let you know that I do not have the correct part with me to fix your machine. I grabbed the wrong bag when loading my van. I've called a colleague across the city who has one, and I will leave now, during my lunch hour, to get it. I'll be back by 1:30 to get the job done. I apologize for my mistake."

- "Sorry for your long wait on hold. I know how frustrating that can be. The reality is that we are having a high number of speaker failures with the new Hubble smartphone. If you'd be willing to take it to the nearest service center, we will swap it for a new one and throw in credit for $20 in new apps. Does that sound OK?"

- "Mr. Customer, I just don't know what the problem is. I've been doing this for four years, I've followed our practices to the letter, and I've gone through all the problem-solving steps. I've checked with headquarters, and they are shaking their heads as well. However, I don't give up. Bear with me on this, and we will figure it out. May I investigate this issue further and get back to you on Thursday?"
- "Mr. Customer, we pride ourselves on building great solutions, but the truth is that we are dealing with very sophisticated products that are part of a very complex system. Things will go wrong at one time or another. That's why you have me! If you'd like, I'll be happy to share with you some of the challenges we can expect to address as we work together."

Brilliant Practice: Use tactful transparency. Let me reiterate again that transparency is based upon integrity. However, it is not an ethical requirement to tell the customer everything you know. For example, refrain from saying:

- "Oh, yeah, that breaks all the time."
- "If you had just looked in your support literature, it would have hit you in the face."
- "Many of our best people left to go to the competition, so the people picking up the phones now don't know much."

Comments such as these add no value and they undermine the customer's trust in your company. Go ahead and think them if you must; just don't say them aloud.

Trust Builder 2: Building Commonality
Building commonality is the sharing of business or personal interests, experiences, or views of the world. People attribute wonderful qualities (that may or may not be real) to those they have

things in common with. The more things in common, the smarter, better looking, and more trustworthy the other person appears.

Let me give you a personal example. In my workshops, I ask people during introductions to share a personal hobby. When I hear someone say, "RVing," I take special mental note, as RVing is a passion of mine. In the corner of my mind I think, *yes, Raul does seem like a clever fellow.* Now, during our break I find out that Raul owns a 40-foot diesel motor home (I have a 40-foot diesel pusher), and something clicks and I think to myself, *he will probably be one of my best students.* If I then find out at lunch that his favorite camping spots are Yellowstone and Glacier National parks (those are my favorites), I begin to assume that Raul is bloody brilliant!

There is no logical connection here, but that is how it works, nonetheless. Since I think I am smart (and good-looking, worldly, debonair, a valuable asset to the planet, and a possessor of many other sterling traits), I assume that someone else who shares my passion must be smart and worldly also. It is strange and illogical, but true. So if you want to build trust, I strongly suggest you look for legitimate things in common with your customers.

> **Flash Point: Potential commonalities are everywhere.**

So where and how do you uncover shared interests and commonalities? They are everywhere, for example:
- **Business.** You may have worked in the same industry, the same company, or the same position.
- **School.** You (or your wife or your son) may have attended the same school that they attended.
- **Organizations.** You may have shared time in the Army, Girl Scouts, Big Brothers, book clubs, MENSA, or the ASPCA.
- **Experiences.** You both may be the eldest child, youngest

child, or middle child; grew up in the city or country; had to walk to school two miles uphill each way; lived in Morocco; hitchhiked across Sweden; survived an earthquake, hurricane, tsunami, flood, or avalanche; climbed every 14teener in Colorado; saw the last game in Yankee Stadium; sat by Bozo the Clown on an airplane; built an airplane; or have kids, grandkids, or common acquaintances.

- **Hobbies and interests.** You may share an enjoyment for golfing, travel, photography, gardening, cooking, bowling, fishing, hiking, cycling, skydiving, flying, reading, snorkeling, swimming, cruising, writing, sports fanning, mountain climbing, whitewater rafting, shortwave radioing, horse racing, rebuilding boat engines, hunting, quilting, coin collecting, shoe shopping, wine tasting, livestock judging, or gourmet hot dog-eating contests. The list is endless.

In fact, commonality is so powerful a factor in building trust that some companies train their salespeople to falsify commonalities that don't exist in order to improve the probability of getting sales![3]

Most people want their business to succeed, and they work hard to contribute to its success. So finding business commonalities is good. However, most people find their passion outside the company walls. The gruff, no-nonsense business exec who has no time to talk service may light up at the mention of scuba diving in the Great Barrier Reef and spend an hour sharing his experiences. The network system manager whose only communication seems to be growls and grunts may chatter like a chipmunk at the mention of grandkids.

Flash Point: Business commonalities are good, but personal commonalities are better.

There are four Brilliant Practices that will help you proactively look for and cultivate areas of common ground. They are Observe, Ask, Keep a Record, and Follow Up. Here are some examples.

Cultivating Commonality: Observe

Here are a few scenarios that can heighten your powers of observation:

- Does your customer have a tattoo on his arm that says, "I love my Harley?" If so, odds are pretty good that this person likes to ride. If you share this pursuit, jump in. A Shining Example would be: "Love your tattoo. I just bought my first Harley three weeks ago and can't wait for the weather to warm up. I've been thinking about going to the big rally in Sturgis this year."
- Most people put reminders of the passions they enjoy in their workspace. A baseball signed by the 1961 Yankees under glass on your customer's desk is a pretty decent indicator of a baseball fan. Your Shining Example comment might be: "Awesome ball! Who signed it?"
- Family pictures on the desk or the wall are a reminder of home. A Shining Example might sound like this: "Is that your daughter? I have a girl about the same age — quite a challenging time to be a parent!"
- Photos of beautiful landscapes are good indicators of a love of travel, photography, or both. Here is a good Shining Example to address your observation: "That looks like the Upper Falls in Yellowstone? What a wonderful place. Did you take that photo?"
- Just walking around the customer's location can yield commonalities to explore. Noticing a companywide love of football might initiate this Shining Example comment: "I noticed a lot of folks in your department appear to be Vikings fans — how about you?"

Examples such as these are simple to employ if you are physically on site at your customer's organization, but if you do most
of your service work over the phone, it is difficult to "observe"
your customer's surroundings. If this is the case, here are two
suggestions: (1) Try to meet with your most important customers face-to-face, and (2) use Skype, FaceTime, or any of the other
video e-services available. Your customer would like to see what
you look like anyway. And if you find several things in common,
your customer will see you as good-looking!

Cultivating Commonality: Ask
Demonstrate initiative and just ask. Most customers open up to
straightforward questions if you sound sincere. Ask things such
as: "What do you like to do when you are not working? Do you
have family? Do you have any plans for the holidays?"

If the customer is tight-lipped or if you'd like to learn more
before meeting the customer, then ask others who know the customer. Maybe you know someone else in that company, or per-
haps one of your sellers or someone else inside or outside your
company may be an acquaintance of your customer and can provide you with information. Furthermore, you could research the
person via LinkedIn or other social media.

Cultivating Commonality: Keep a Record
If building trust from commonality is important (it is), then unless you have a great memory (most of us don't), write down
what you learn. You will be writing down your notes from a
service call or a customer meeting anyway, so just make a few
notes about the person at the same time. Your notes don't have to
be elaborate or complex, just hobbies and interests or important
things going on in your customer's life.

For example, you might have jotted down a note like this:
John has one son and two daughters. Oldest daughter just accepted to State on academic scholarship. He loves hiking in the

summer and skiing in the winter. Hopes to go to Yellowstone this August.

Cultivating Commonality: Follow Up
Before each planned conversation, take 30 seconds and review your notes on the customer. Unless you are dealing with a no-nonsense, no-time-to-chat issue, start each conversation around a topic the customer is interested in and that you have in common. A Shining Example would sound like this: "John, before we get down to business, how did your daughter's graduation go?" Or, "I just checked The Weather Channel a few minutes ago—20 inches of powder is predicted for Vail! Bet I know where you are heading Friday."

Go the extra kilometer. On areas of commonality, send the customer information of interest. You might pen a personal note that reads like this Shining Example: "I really enjoyed our conversation about butterflies the other day. I didn't know if you saw this, but attached is a wonderful story about the Mexico Monarch migration. I hope to go someday. Enjoy!" Or you could send an e-mail that says: "Regarding our conversation about the World Cup, you were right, of course! Brazil is the only country to have participated in every World Cup finals tournament. Here is the link: http://en.wikipedia.org/wiki/List_of_FIFA_World_Cup_finals."

Trust Builder 3: Showing Respect
Respect is evidenced by practicing common courtesy plus understanding and valuing the uniqueness of the customer, including different opinions and ideas.

Brilliant Practice: Respect the customer's time. The BSP practices common courtesy by respecting the customer's time. The BSP is punctual; if she says she will call at 10 a.m., she calls at 10 a.m., not 10:07 a.m. or 9:53 a.m. If given 15 minutes for a meeting, the BSP is done within 14 minutes. The BSP plans for things that might slow him down and allows for unexpected traffic, current work that goes over the expected time frame he has allotted, interruptions in his day, and so on. When appropriate, the BSP prepares an agenda to help keep conversations focused on what is most important. This helps to demonstrate that he values the customer's time.

Shining Examples that show respect of your customer's time constraints are:

- "Bill, when we set up this call you said that you had a hard stop at 11:30 a.m. Is that still the case, or have things changed? Fine, I will make sure I am out the door by 11:29."
- "Susan, I am calling from my car. I left an hour early antici-pating heavy traffic, but I didn't expect crazy-heavy traffic. It will take me at least another 40 minutes to get there. I want to respect your time—should I come when I can, or should we reschedule?"
- (E-mail): "I am looking forward to our conference call Tues-day at 9 a.m. Eastern. I want to make sure that we adequate-ly cover the items most important to you, so I've attached a draft agenda for you to review. Please let me know if you have any changes or ideas so that we are sure to make the most of our time together."

Brilliant Practice: Respect the customer's communication style. Some people like to look at the forest; others prefer to study the trees. It is a sign of respect when you learn and align with the customer's communication style, even if it is not comfortable for you. A Shining Example might sound like this: "From our last conversation, I observed that you are a big-picture person, cor-rect? I have a 20-page document that gets into the details of the planned project, but I thought you might prefer starting with this one slide I put together showing the key points of the entire sys-tem."

Brilliant Practice: Respect decorum. You are a reflection of your company. Respect decorum and respect yourself by being neat and clean, polished and groomed. Dress appropriately. I'll cover more on appearance under Trust Builder 5: Exhibiting Credibility.

Brilliant Practice: Respect the background and experience of the customer. You may have to deal with customers who have different career backgrounds than you have, and thus lack your experience and expertise. For example, you may need to talk to nontechnical business managers about your products and services. Show respect by using your customer acumen (discussed in Chapter 3) to talk in terms that they can understand and relate to. You may deal with people from countries with very different cultures than your own. Anything you do that shows you care about these cultural differences is a big plus. Taking the time to learn a few key words and phrases in your customer's native tongue, demonstrating familiarity with their country's history and traditions, or showing you have an understanding of their cultural protocol will be very much appreciated.

Shining Examples include comments such as these:

- "In doing research on your company, I know that improving the satisfaction of your customers is a top priority. If you'd like, I can explain how upgrading to the new system can do just that. I think it will make your job as sales leader easier as well."
- "Mr. Customer, I am afraid that jargon tends to dominate much of the conversations I am involved in. Sometimes we even confuse ourselves with acronyms and abbreviations! I try hard to avoid it, but would you please let me know if I say something that may not make sense? May I do the same of you?"
- "Ms. Customer, I hope that I don't sound aggressive, but I bet we'd both like to have this project completed before the European summer holiday season begins. Trying to get appointments in Greece in July is like trying to get tickets to the

World Cup a week before the opening match."

Brilliant Practice: Respect the uniqueness of the customer, including different opinions and ideas. In a time of growing global intolerance, it is refreshing when people value uniqueness and are open to concepts different from their own. The BSP works hard at understanding the customer and respecting the customer's thinking even though it may be much different than that of the BSP. What at first you might consider lousy, stupid, or crazy thinking can have some merit if tolerated and respected.

Shining Examples that show respect of your customer's uniqueness include:

- "Yes, I had heard that Al Gore invented the Internet."
- "OK, that makes sense. I see how you came to the conclusion that not downloading the security patches would make you more secure. Looks like it would help if our manual was clearer."
- "Oh, now I understand. You connected the alajo to the caryanter via the worm inverter. That's really creative. I have never seen that before!"

Trust Builder 4: Creating Likeability

Quite simply, creating likeability means being enjoyable to work with. Here is a difficult quiz: Whom would you prefer to spend the day with: (1) a pleasant, enthusiastic mate who shares your love of travel and photography and always insists on buying lunch at Antonio's, or (2) a nasty-looking bloke with an annoying twitch who constantly talks about all his woes and will only eat at a fast-food burger chain? If the bar exam had questions this easy, we'd all be lawyers. Given a choice, we will always choose the more likeable person to work or play with. Here are some Brilliant Practices that create likeability:

- This is an easy one: Just practice the other trust builders! When you are seen as being transparent, sharing commonalities, showing respect, being credible, and acting reliably, people like you more. For example, if you "man up when you screw up," your transparency will be appreciated and people will like you more for it.

- Smile a lot. Lead with a welcoming and sincere smile…and keep smiling. Research shows that the more you smile, the more people like you.[4]
- Display positive body language. Keep your head up, make eye contact, use open gestures with your hands and arms.
- Use words that convey welcome and openness.[5] Positive phrases such as "nice to see you," or "glad you are here" make you more likeable.
- Use words that display helpfulness.[6] Statements such as "how can I help?", "what can I do?", "gladly with pleasure," "absolutely," and "sure" work magic if spoken sincerely.
- Let the other person talk. The customer (like the majority of the global population) likes to talk. Let her do it, and you will be liked for not interrupting.

Trust Builder 5: Exhibiting Credibility

When you are able to demonstrate competence to your customer, you quickly build your credibility. In the service world, credibility is best demonstrated by possessing appropriate credentials, sharing relevant experience, and exuding confidence.

Appropriate Credentials

Because technical proficiency is an important part of most service jobs, having proven technical competency is important, and credentials are a way to assure the customer that you, or your team, have it. Especially for the technically oriented customer, having certifications within your team is a must.

Brilliant Practice: Let others do your bragging. Use relevant customer testimonials to demonstrate credibility. If you are new to a customer, have someone else (your boss or your boss' boss) introduce your competence. Have them send a resume highlighting areas of importance to the customer. If your boss is not a good writer, write it for her.

Some Shining Examples include:

- "Please don't take our word for it. May I share with you some testimonials from customers we worked with facing similar challenges?"
- "Our customers tell us that what makes our organization special is our drive for perfection."
- (Letter or e-mail): "Dear Mr. Customer, I am pleased to introduce you to your new FSE, Tommy Zee. I have attached his bio. As you will see, Tommy has strong technical know-how, graduating third in his class at TopNotch Technical College. He has had three years of solid performance as an aviation service pro in the Army. He has certifications in A+ and has successfully completed our extensive and intensive training program. I think you will be very pleased with his performance. Expect an introductory call from him this Thursday."

Relevant Experience
Sharing your personal experiences, or the experiences of your team or your company, is important in proving to the customer that you can handle his problems. The more experience you have with companies of similar type and size, and those within the same industry or marketplace, the more relevant you are to the customer.

Brilliant Practice: Demonstrate your experience with customer examples that your customer can relate to.

Here are three Shining Examples:

- "Thank you for sharing that background information. I feel I have a good understanding of your current situation and what you want to accomplish. Mind if I share an example of a customer I worked with that had a similar issue?"
- "Over the last 15 years I've orchestrated preventive maintenance during plant shutdowns many times. May I share with

you what I have learned that will ensure things go smoothly?"
- "I had the pleasure of working with another innovative company like yours that switched over from Giganzo Business Intelligence Software to ours, and they did it within 30 days. Would you like to hear their story?"

Exuding Confidence
The brilliant service professional communicates confidence in everything she says and does, and in how she appears. The BSP considers all indicators of competence, because when dealing with the intangible, people look for tangible things that they feel are indicators of competence and quality. In the world of services, the brand walks around on two feet.[7] Is your appearance consistent with what the customer would assume a brilliant service professional should look like? How you present yourself makes a difference. How about your briefcase or handbag? Your promotional literature? Your vehicle? Do you walk and talk like a professional? The customer takes all this in and makes assumptions, correctly or incorrectly, from what they see. Here are some Brilliant Practices that will help you exude confidence:
- Rigorously prepare for each conversation or encounter. If the conversation is not important enough to warrant preparation, don't have it. If it is important, practice what you will say for each conversation. Contemplate questions you might ask and consider the questions you might be asked. Think about concerns the customer may have and how you might respond. Being prepared has a calming effect that people read as, "this guy knows his stuff." More on this in Chapter 7.
- Be conscious of what your body communicates. Keep your head high and your posture erect but not stiff. Walk with a purposeful gait like a mountain lion stalking prey. Keep your motion fluid and your smile at the ready. Look people in the eye when you speak. Pause before speaking. Be serious but passionate, focused but relaxed, animated but controlled.

- Dress like the confident professional you are. I am not pre-suming to know what is ideal for your situation. Whatever the attire, be clean and neat (person, clothing, vehicle, office, handbag). It may not be necessary for you to regularly wear a suit and tie (although sometimes it might), but maybe a button-down shirt, slacks, and loafers are more appropriate than a Grateful Dead T-shirt and Teva sandals (yes, even in Silicon Valley). Most of the time, gray hair is a plus, so no need to dye it!
- Speak carefully. Like a star witness for the defense, the BSP pauses and thinks before speaking, knowing that every word counts and might be remembered.
- Write carefully. Take your time! Write for clarity and pur-pose; grammar and spelling count.
- Attempt to understand your customer's unique perceptions. Remember that what is important to one customer may not be important to another. Study your customer to best un-derstand what he would see as credible. Shining Examples that will help you uncover your customer's point of view include: "Tell me, Mr. Customer, what does the ideal consul-tant look like to you?" Or "Ms. Customer, you work with lots of service providers. From your perspective, what do the best ones do that others don't?"
- Be positive, but don't confuse confidence with enthusiasm — confidence is contagious; enthusiasm may not be.

Trust Builder 6: Demonstrating Reliability
Consistently doing what you say you will do — when you say you will do it and how you say you will do it — demonstrates your reliability. Being dependable is always valued, but how many people do you know that you can count on no matter what? The more the customer views what you do as important, and the more potential risk they perceive if things go wrong, the more vital reliability is toward building trust.

Brilliant Practice: Think deeply before committing. As the Danish proverb states, eggs and oaths are easily broken. Before you give your word, be sure you won't break it. Personally, I have found out the hard way that it takes me two to three times longer to do most things than I anticipate. How about you?

A Shining Example in this instance would sound like this: "Mr. Customer, my first reaction is to say yes. However, I know myself too well, and I sometimes overcommit. I don't want to do that to you. I'd like to look at my schedule and my plans first before I respond. May I get back to you this afternoon?"

Brilliant Practice: Only commit to what you can control. Even if the word "manager" is in your title, you don't really direct the actions of others, do you? As a services professional, there are very few things that we have direct control over. We only manage ourselves. We are effective by our ability to influence.

Here's a Shining Example to support this Brilliant Practice: "Mr. Customer, I understand. If I were in your shoes, I'd want a set date when I know the issue will be totally resolved. Unfortunately, I can't give you that date today. Several key people inside our company must be involved, and I don't control their workload, vacation schedule, or if they will get ill. I only commit to what I can control. I will, however, commit to the following...."

Brilliant Practice: Think small. Psychologically, fulfilling a small promise "counts" as much as fulfilling a big promise. Therefore, actively looking for small commitments to demonstrate your reliability is a good way to build the track record necessary to be seen as reliable. The same holds true for not meeting a small promise—it may not seem like a big deal to you if your promised update is only a day late, and the customer will rarely mention it, but deep down the customer takes note of the unreliability.

This is a Shining Example for "thinking small": "Mr. Customer, my colleague at our company wrote a white paper on this very topic. Would you like to read it? I will send it to you tomorrow morning by noon." Then tomorrow morning at 11:57 a.m., you send the article with these words in the e-mail: "Mr. Customer, as promised, here is the article I mentioned yesterday. I think you will especially enjoy the two paragraphs I highlighted. I look forward to your comments the next time we talk."

Flash Point: The dogma of "under-promise and over-deliver" is usually a bad idea when trying to demonstrate reliability.

Brilliant Practice: To demonstrate reliability, do what you said you would do, exactly when you said you would do it. The concept of under-promise and over-deliver sounds sexy, but if followed, it lowers your reliability in the customer's eyes. For example, let's say that you have told the customer that you will have his requested analysis to him in seven days. Let's assume that the customer thinks this is reasonable because he believes it will take some critical thinking to deliver something of value on this issue that has perplexed him for months.

Now, let's say you get the analysis to the customer in two days. On the outside, he will probably smile and say thank you for the fast turnaround. But on the inside, the customer might be thinking: *That guy didn't know enough about the issue to know how long it should take. I wonder about his experience? He must have just thrown something together to get it off his plate. I wonder about his commitment? Was he trying to impress me by under-promising and over-delivering? I see that as deceitful.*

Those are not good thoughts, are they? So what will the customer probably think the next time you make a promise—for instance, doing something within 10 days? Probably something like this: *Well, he hedged several days last time, so I guess I should expect his response in three or four days this time.*

If you do get what you committed to do done in three or four days, you have confirmed that what you say is not what to expect. If you complete it in the 10 days stated, the customer will not know what to think. Either way, your reliability is damaged (and probably your credibility).

Let me reiterate: If you are trying to demonstrate reliability, do the job as close to what you described and as close to when you promised as you can.

There is one important exception to this, however. If you are dealing with something of high importance to the customer — for example, lives in danger — you ethically owe it to the customer to deliver the goods at the quality level that is appropriate as soon as possible.

Here is a Shining Example that demonstrates reliability: "I understand the criticality of your situation, and I promise to do what I can to bring resolution as soon as I can. As you know, this is complex and will involve several of our best and busiest people. I will start immediately after our conversation. As a realistic estimate, based upon my experience, this will probably take three to five days. However, if the stars align and the gears mesh, of course we will do it sooner. Tell me, how would you like me to update you on the status?"

Trust Builder 7: Maintaining Contact
Interacting with your customer on a regular basis allows you to build a trust-based, quality relationship. Absence may make the heart grow fonder in your personal life, but it doesn't work that way in business! Assuming that your customer interactions were positive, the more contact you have with your customer, the more trust you will build. Who in your organization has more contact with customers than service professionals? No one. So make these interactions count.

Brilliant Practice: Schedule contacts. Schedule dates to contact all customers you want to build/maintain trust with. Actively look for value-adding things (business or personal) to contact the customer about. Once a day, once a week, once a month, or once a quarter, make sure you have made contact.

These Shining Examples are good illustrations of ways to schedule contact and foster commonality at the same time:

- (Voice message): "Mr. Customer, this is Max from Bellenti. My purpose for calling is to make sure that the machine I replaced parts on last week is still performing up to specifications. There is no reason to call back if it is, unless you want to talk about the Sunday Bears game! Thank you."

- (E-mail): "Hello Bill, nothing new on this end business-wise that I know of, but I wanted to confirm that you are pleased with the results of our last engagement. Please let me know if you have any questions or ideas. By the way, I found a great price on tickets, so we are heading out to Denver to visit our grandkids on the 20th."

The Law of Intermingleability

As you have already realized, the really cool thing is that all of the trust builders link, build, mesh, and intermingle with one another. Your transparency shows respect and makes you more likeable. Demonstrating reliability positively impacts your credibility, and so on. The effect goes beyond being additive, to being synergetic.

To gain the desired results of repeatable, sustainable service performance requires that you apply the seven trust-building behaviors. In our next chapter, I will introduce an important enabler of these behaviors: customer acumen.

CHAPTER 3

Customer Acumen
The Brilliant Differentiator

In this chapter, I define customer acumen and explain why having it is so important. Next, I explain the different types of business issues that form a large part of customer acumen and demonstrate how they impact customer focus and customer decision making. Then, I share a number of possible ways for you to build your customer acumen and become savvier about your customers, your customers' markets, and business in general. Along the way, I introduce you to T-People, and share Brilliant Practices and Shining Examples.

What Is Customer Acumen?

What is customer acumen? Customer acumen is having a good knowledge of your customers, understanding the environment in which your customers operate, and being savvy about business in general. As you will soon see, it requires knowledge, familiarity, and experience in many things, and thus takes time to develop.

Why Customer Acumen Is So Important

As I referenced in the Introduction and in Chapter 1, service professionals who possess customer acumen deliver more value to the customers they serve and to the company they work for. Their ability to connect the dots, to explain how their company's offerings can positively impact customers in ways they understand and care about, is a big deal. Only a small percentage of service professionals have strong customer acumen, hence this rarity is even more important. Like a white calf among a heard of Black Angus, customer acumen allows you to stand out from the herd of other services providers.

Here is a personal example of customer acumen: I enjoy photography. If I have a technical question about a Canon lens, I can call Canon technical support and usually get a solid answer, as they have strong technical acumen regarding their products. However, if I ask that person about how that lens compares with a similar Nikon or Sony lens, I probably won't get much help. However, if I call B&H, the definitive source for imaging technology, they will give me lens comparison information across brands. In addition, they'll provide me with knowledgeable insight as to the specific application of each lens, such as which one is best for bird photography. I highly value their customer acumen and thus give them a great deal of my business.

Jim Spohrer, who both started and headed up the Service Research Unit at IBM, offers up another example of the importance of customer acumen. Mr. Spohrer was speaking at a services conference I attended. During his presentation he was asked what his service research biggest challenge was in helping IBM to be successful. His reply: Creating T-People. Of course the next question from the audience was, what is a T-Person?

He explained that IBM has a great many people who are experts in some aspect of technology. These are very valuable folks, as it takes six to ten years to gain depth in any field. He stated that in the old days, when customers' technology executives made the technology decisions for their organizations, all was fine because both the customer in charge and the IBM experts spoke the same language. But as customer executives from all disciplines became involved in technology decisions, IBM staff who possessed only technical depth were unable to communicate with customer executives from other parts of their business.

In today's landscape, IBM needs people who not only understand the technology and can talk with chief information officers and chief technology officers; they also need the business knowledge necessary to speak to chief financial officers, chief marketing officers, chief executive officers, and so on.[1] They need to be deep, but they also have to be wide. Hence, the T-People label was born, driven by the need for both technical expertise and business know-how across disciplines, as seen in Figure 3.1.

My guess is that your organization needs and values customer acumen as well.

Figure 3.1

Flash Point: The greater your customer acumen, the more you can anticipate the business impact of your recommendations on your customer.

You can't be taught business acumen in one dose of reading, listening, or training. It is much too diverse to learn in any lecture, course, or even in an MBA program. You have to learn it yourself. I will, however, try to point you in the right direction.

Understanding Business Issues

The core ingredient of having strong customer acumen is having a good understanding of business issues. Business issues are the drivers of how organizations build their strategy, determine their goals, allocate resources, purchase technologies, and do most everything else. The four business issues are market forces, industry regulations, organization challenges, and department imperatives. The interesting thing, as seen in Figure 3.2, is that these four business issues are linked: Market forces plus indus-

Figure 3.2

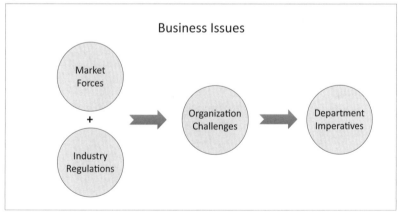

try regulations drive organization challenges, which determine department imperatives.

Here is an explanation of each of these business issues, along with some examples.

Market Forces

Market forces are the big and broad impactors of the business world. They are as varied as tourists on the beach and can brighten your day or burn your skin. Current economic conditions and future projections can cause caution or exuberance in the boardroom. The availability and cost of critical inputs (e.g., talent, capital, raw materials) may limit the range of strategic options that businesses can consider. Existing and expected interest rates often shape the speed and scope of investment. Potential killer technologies might offer threats to the kings and hope for the peasants. Climate change, political upheaval, inflation, deflation, currency exchange rates, stock market prices, and consumer confidence all have the potential to impact businesses globally, regionally, and locally.

Industry Regulations

All industries have requirements that participating organizations must meet. Numerous regulatory organizations provide standards touching all aspects of the enterprise, including worker health, plant safety, individual privacy, product quality, and guidelines on pricing. Sometimes there are new regulations, deregulations, or re-regulations that may have minor or major significance. Changes in industry requirements can create barriers to entry, keeping potential customers out. Or changes in regulation can tear down these barriers, opening up brand-new competitors. All of these requirements impact cost and create or lessen opportunities.

Organization Challenges

The market forces tempered by the industry regulations described above have significant impact on the problems and opportunities facing a business and, hence, drive the organization strategy and plans. Here are some examples of possible organizational challenges: Extreme negative market forces such as a recession may make the very survival of the business an organization imperative. New regulations may open the gates for mergers, and thus acquiring a competitor could become an organization priority. Rallying share price, improving the corporate image, increasing market share, growing the business, boosting profitability, driving innovation, differentiating from the competition, improving cash flow, increasing security, or improving output are examples.

Initiatives are then developed to address those organization challenges. An emphasis on quality might be created in an attempt to improve product reliability and enhance customer satisfaction. A cost-cutting campaign might be started in an attempt to boost profitability and bolster share price. A savvy business leader might make big investments in building services capabilities to sell more products and create competitive differentiation.

Department Imperatives

If your organization is well run, and I am sure it is, priorities trickle down, hence the challenges of top management become the imperatives of departments such as IT, finance, marketing, services, engineering, and so on.

Here are some examples of how this can work:

1. The availability of low-cost money coupled with modest growth projections for a particular industry may spur a company to ramp up new product development. Executives might decide to make a large investment in a state-of-the-art facility capable of utilizing an emerging technology — one that might fuel new, innovative products in two or three years. In this scenario, the head of manufacturing will probably be focused on overseeing the planning and building of this facility and delegate other tasks until the facility is up

and running smoothly. The head of finance might be given key performance indicators on securing favorable funding. The head of IT may be very actively involved, attempting to research, source, and lead the implementation of necessary technology that will not only provide the greatest bang for the buck, but also integrate well with the overall information systems. IT will probably have a significant budget for a project of this size and business importance. For the heads of most other functions, this initiative will probably have little impact on their priorities, unless their budgets are reduced in order to help fund the new facility.

2. Imagine that projected weak growth and financial uncertainty coupled with pending expensive industry regulation may cause a hunker-down mentality among top management of a business, thus instigating a hiring freeze and cost-cutting mandate. Under this gloom-and-doom administration, everything is on hold. The only investments that this sky-is-falling group might consider are those targeted to increase efficiencies that have a guaranteed one-year payback.

3. After considering a number of strategic options, a large ERP software company with mature products in a mature industry may decide to build services capabilities to differentiate itself from the competition. In this case, the executive responsible for services has the spotlight on her. It will take major investments in the services business (talent, processes, knowledge management) to pull this off. A savvy services leader knows that dealing with the product culture will be the biggest challenge to success, so that will be the top priority.

In this case, the services executive most likely will actively seek the special expertise of firms that know what it takes to aggressively grow services capabilities inside a technology company. At the same time, the business development group will be building or buying capabilities to make this ambition a reality. The head of IT may support the acquisition of customer relationship management (CRM) and/or other knowledge management (KM) technologies. The head of sales may have been given the directive to train his sellers on selling services. Marketing might start allocating time and budget to developing campaigns touting the value advantage that the new services will bring the customer.

As you have seen, department imperatives will vary across the board. Here are a few other common examples:

- Adding talent to meet new demand.
- Motivating an overworked team.
- Doing more with less.
- Retaining more customers.
- Improving utilization.
- Changing compensation.
- Boosting productivity.
- Changing roles and responsibilities.
- Streamlining processes.
- Reorganizing.
- Increasing uptime.
- Retaining star players.
- Cutting costs.
- Improving safety.
- Adopting new technologies.
- Increasing security.
- Outsourcing.
- Improving channel relationships.
- Handling the merging.
- Acquiring or being acquired.
- Driving efficiencies.
- Speeding new product introductions.
- Transitioning from free to fee.
- Changing the culture.
- Compressing cycle time.

Flash Point: Rarely does a cool technology trigger a major purchase or change in business operation. It is the business issues that trigger the technical needs (Figure 3.3).

Figure 3.3

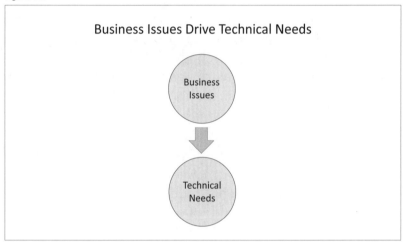

Building Customer Acumen: Brilliant Practices

The good news is that there are a gazillion resources that can help you build your customer acumen, and many are free. The bad news is, like the champagne brunch at The Ritz-Carlton, because there are so many possibilities, determining where to start may seem overwhelming. Let me share some proven Brilliant Practices.

To Strengthen Your Knowledge of Your Customers and Your Customers' Industries

There are many ways to become more knowledgeable about your customers and their industries. Following these Brilliant

Practices will set you apart from your services peers.

- Absorb annual reports. Public companies in many countries are required by law to publicly file an annual report, 99 percent of which is focused on financials. The really great thing is that almost every annual report begins with a few succinct pages from the tip-top executives summarizing the past year and discussing business issues and industry trends. This is followed by an outline of the coming year's priorities and the strategic initiatives formulated to accomplish these goals. In just a few minutes, a thoughtful reader can learn significant insights into the executive imperatives. If you have dedicated accounts, downloading and studying the executive summaries of their annual reports is mandatory.

- Attend industry conferences. As you know, there are conferences for every industry. If your products are targeted at telecommunications, go to telecommunications conferences. Focus on the presentations, workshops, and roundtables that talk about the business side of things. Proactively talk to the people you meet and ask them about their business and their business issues. Along with getting more business savvy, you are professionally representing your company and making industry contacts.

- Attend services industry conferences. Since you are a service professional, it makes sense that you learn more about the services industry. These symposiums are attended primarily by service and support executives and managers, and most of the presentations, roundtables, and discussions focus on the business side of services. You will learn the business issues and industry trends impacting services businesses. Attend these conferences, learn about business, find out how other services businesses work, make contacts, and have fun.

- Join and participate in trade associations. Trade associations are usually nonprofits headed by boards of volunteer executives who are passionate about their industry. If you are excited about that industry, join and volunteer. Not only will you learn a lot, but you will be in close association with the movers and shakers in your industry.

- Use social media. As you know, there are scores of social media options, but for most of us, LinkedIn is the most valuable. Find some customer-specific or business-oriented LinkedIn groups that you find interesting and follow the conversations. You don't have to participate, just observe.
- Ride with brilliant sales professionals. Your company's very best sales professionals are masters at customer acumen. You can learn a huge amount from them in a short time if you have the opportunity to see them in action. Once you have gotten the OK to spend a few days with a sales pro, follow this approach:
  1. Pre-work: Find out what accounts you will be seeing with the sales star. Access your company's knowledge management system to learn about the account. Download the annual reports of the customers you are going to visit and study the remarks of the senior executives.
  2. Pre-call: Over breakfast and on the drive to the customer site, quiz the seller. Ask about the customer's background, goals, issues, and concerns. Learn what the seller is trying to accomplish, why she is trying to accomplish it, and the hoped-for impact on the customer. Also, discuss how the seller will introduce you. I'd suggest telling the truth! "Sammy is one of our service professionals. He is interested in learning more about our customers' businesses and asked if he could ride along with me to listen and observe. Is that OK with you?" My experience has been that the customer thinks it is really cool.
  3. During the call: Be quiet! Intently observe the customer-seller interaction. Learn. Jot down a few notes if it is comfortable to do so.
  4. Post-call: Ask the seller how it went, her summary of the

conversation, and her planned next steps. Further, ask why she is choosing this path of action with her customer and what she bases her recommendation on.

5. Throughout the whole process, practice the seven trust builders. Not only will you learn a tremendous amount, but you will be building a relationship with a key internal player. After a few hours of showing interest and respect, the sales star will do the same to you. She will ask about your role and the value you bring—which is very powerful, as it spreads the gospel of services.

- Attend sales meetings. The same insights and benefits you gain while riding with a sales pro apply when attending sales meetings. After you have attended a few of these gatherings, your input will be invited and you probably will be asked to present your viewpoint. Again, you are getting smarter and building important relationships as you go.

- Talk regularly with the sales folks. It's a great idea to have regular contact with the sellers who have the accounts you service. If you are currently not invited, be proactive and get yourself invited. Explain that you want to know the sellers' plans so that you can support them and avoid the very awkward situation of not having one voice with the customer. Give them an overview of what you are doing with your accounts, and offer a heads-up regarding any potential problems or potential sales opportunities. You need them on your team, and once they see the value you can bring, they will want you on their team.

- Participate in lunch-and-learn sessions. Hey, you gotta eat lunch anyway—might as well learn something. I know many of you participate in lunch-and-learns, however, most of those are focused on technology. Once per month, why not do a customer acumen session? For example, invite a finance executive to participate and ask him how he makes financial decisions for his business. Invite your vice president of sales to share industry issues and trends. For the price of a balo-ney-and-cheese sandwich, a bag of chips, and a can of Coke, you can get smarter about business the easy way.

- Attend briefings put on by your company. Many companies, especially big ones, have all-hands meetings that are open to everyone and share a big-picture view of what is going on. Furthermore, some companies hold regular briefings for analysts that you might be able to dial in to. Take advantage of these.

To Better Understand Business in General

These Brilliant Practices will sharpen your general business acumen, making you more knowledgeable and insightful when connecting the dots for your customers.

- Read or listen to books, magazines, journals, newspapers, webcasts, podcasts, or blogs having to do with business. Anything addressing an important aspect of business that is backed by research, supported by experience, and well written can be a powerful way to build customer acumen. Most all webcasts and podcasts are complimentary, and most all news websites offer at least partial access for free. For example, I used to subscribe to *The Wall Street Journal* online, but I have found that just scanning the headlines each morning is a great way to stay abreast of general business news. If I find something of high interest, I research it elsewhere.
- Give speeches, do webcasts, lead lunch-and-learns. Why not? If your company sells security software, give a presentation on "The Five Things Every CEO Should Know About Internet Security." If your company builds genome-mapping equipment, "The Business Implications of DNA" would be a great topic.
- Take university business courses or sign up for seminars and workshops either in person or face-to-face. Many quality business courses are taught online asynchronously. There-

fore, you can participate when and where you want. There is nothing like learning in your pajamas. Furthermore, iTunes University and many other universities are now opening up some courses for free.

- Write articles. There are hundreds of online publications always looking for quality content. As you start to get proficient in some aspect of business, share it with others.
- Blog. Post comments on other writers' blogs when you have something of value to add. Consider starting your own blog once you begin mastering some element of business.
- Be mentored. If you can find the right person, this is a powerful way to get business smarts.

Guidelines for Building Customer Acumen

Here are some guidelines for increasing your level of customer acumen. Many of the steps are quite simple and take just a small commitment of your time, while others are larger in scope, but ultimately the payoff for your dedication is big.

- **Pick a topic you find interesting and start there.** Years ago when I embarked on my customer acumen journey, I chose strategy as my initial focus—something I found interesting. If I had chosen finance at that crucial time in my career, I'd probably be a plumber today instead of a services strategist.
- **Do some research up front.** There's a ton of good stuff out there on building both your business and your customer acumen skills, but it isn't always easy to find. Find people who are business savvy, whose opinion you respect, and ask them what sources they recommend.[2]
- **Take small bites.** Set aside 20 minutes a day, five days a week, and you will be talking business speak in style within three months!
- **Make it easy.** If you have chosen to follow a blog authored

by one of your customers, set up an RSS feed so the information comes to you. The same goes for podcasts that automatically download onto your device.

- **Have a buddy.** If you have a colleague who also wants to advance his career, work together. Share information of value. Talk every couple of weeks. It will make things easier and more fun.

- **Start a book club.** Find out what books your company's executives or your customers' executives are reading and meet with like-minded peers once a week, either in person or virtually, to discuss the entire book or a chapter. Ask each person to comment on key issues and their potential impact. For example, many years ago I was heading a small consulting firm that employed very smart people, but they knew nothing about business. I bought them all Peter Drucker's classic management book, *Management: Tasks, Responsibilities, Practices,*[3] and assigned them one chapter per week to read. Each week I asked them to answer three questions: (1) What three things did you find most interesting? (2) What questions do you have? (3) How can we apply what we have learned to make our business better? We would discuss the answers each Friday over lunch (I bought the pizza). Small investment, big return.

- **Tap into your company's resources.** Many businesses have libraries that loan out materials, including relevant magazines and journals and complimentary online learning. Furthermore, some companies have programs that will pay for all or part of your learning, including degree programs. Take advantage of it.

- **Build it into your personal development plan at work.** Committing to something to your boss in writing can be quite motivating! You will be rewarded for something that you should do anyway.

- **Double-dip.** For example, when you workout, listen to a business book while you are exercising. When you commute, read or listen to something that makes you smarter about business. Let's say your spouse is starting a new business for building and maintaining websites. You could focus on learning more about marketing while you exercise, and then share what you learn over dinner to help your spouse market her business better. Double-dipping is the most efficient thing you can do.

- **Double-dip really big.** Depending on your career goals, you could do an online master's degree program in some aspect of business. This will not only greatly increase your business knowledge, but the degree will beef up your credentials and build your personal brand. In addition, you will probably create some valuable relationships along the way.

Having solid customer acumen can distinguish you from your colleagues. Build upon that knowledge and master the four core relationship skills presented in the next chapter, and you will become one value-creating machine.

CHAPTER 4

The Four Core
Relationship Skills

In this chapter, I introduce the four core relationship skills required of the brilliant service professional. They are:

1. **Listening with Intensity.** The BSP knows that listening is vital—actively hearing and understanding not only the facts regarding the customer's situation, but the personal feelings the customer has about them.

2. **Probing with Purpose.** The BSP uses the right probe at the right time in the right way to best understand the customer's situation and to help the customer see things in a different light.

3. **Presenting Powerfully.** Once the brilliant service pro has a clear understanding of the customer's situation, he powerfully presents his recommendations, explaining "the what," "the why," and "the benefit" to the customer.

4. **Acknowledging Concerns.** The BSP lets the customer know he understands and cares how the customer feels—a necessary first step in earning the right to address the facts.

In addition, I also introduce the Customer Emotion Meter and discuss the special challenge of being experienced and really smart. Again, Brilliant Practices and Shining Examples will help you apply these skills directly to your situation.

Flash Point: Relationship skills are learnable!

Listening with Intensity

This skill is not called listening for understanding, or listening with intent, or listening with curiosity…it is called listening with INTENSITY!

I am certain that in scenarios in which you have a very high interest in the subject matter, you do listen with intensity, hanging on every word, grasping the nuances of tone, absorbing the body language of the other person. Yet, listening with intensity is hard! One has to maintain total focus and give the customer 100 percent attention, 100 percent of the time. Personally, I find I need to expend a lot of effort to deliver on this mission.

During my conversations, other business tries to sneak into my mind, taking away my focus. For no conscious reason, I might find myself wondering if an aperture of $f/14$ might be better than $f/22$ in capturing sunrises on the beach, or hoping that the barbecued ribs on tonight's menu are moist enough, or for no reason at all I might become fixated on the nose of the customer I am talking with. There is a tendency in all of us for our minds to wander or to get distracted. Furthermore, there are lots of other barriers to listening with intensity.

In this section, I list the common barriers to listening that we face every day, followed by Brilliant Practices and a few Shining Examples, where appropriate, for overcoming them.

Barrier to Listening: Limited Hearing Ability

Hearing loss caused by years of attending rock concerts, serving on submarines, or just getting older can obviously be a big barrier to listening.

Brilliant Practice: Accept it. Seek professional help, get the best hearing aids available, and learn how to optimize hearing performance.

Here are a couple of Shining Examples that address this barrier to listening:

- "Doc, I'm tired of missing out on conversations. Fit me with the best hearing aids you've got."
- "Thomas, let me explain why I moved to this chair. All those Navy years of loading ordinance on fighters on the deck of aircraft carriers took its toll on my hearing. I have hearing aids, but I find I hear best when I'm situated this way."

Barrier to Listening: Physical State of Health

If you are exhausted from lack of sleep, ill from the flu, or recovering from brain surgery, you may not have the necessary energy or capacity to listen well.

Brilliant Practice: Schedule conversations when you will be rested, alert, and ready to focus. When that is not possible, either postpone your meeting to a later time or have someone else hold the conversation for you. If you have to perform, minimize your energy requirements — shorten the conversations or spread conversations out so you can rest in between.

Here are a few Shining Examples to use when you're under the weather:

- "Natalie, I am not myself right now. I had surgery Tuesday and I find I am not 100 percent yet. Therefore, I've asked my boss, Stan, to stand in for our afternoon call. Or, if you can wait, I'd be happy to reschedule for tomorrow or the day after. Which do you prefer?"
- "Bill, I am looking forward to talking with you today. If your

schedule allows, I'd like to move our call from 3 p.m. to 4 p.m. If that won't work for you, no problem."
- "Henry, with your permission, I'd like to keep our 11 a.m. call to 20 minutes. I always appreciate your focus and succinctness, so I think 20 minutes will be plenty. OK with you?"

Barrier to Listening: Inhibiting Environment
Your environment may have lousy acoustics, loud air conditioners, barking dogs, noisy traffic, screaming babies, or multiple conversations happening at once, all of which make it difficult to hear, let alone listen to what your customer is saying. If your place of work sounds like a practice field during an artillery drill, you are fighting a losing battle. In a case such as this, sound retreat and regroup.

Brilliant Practice: Move to a quieter area; one free of distractions, and create your own zone (or cone) of silence.

Shining Examples that address this type of situation include:
- "Brian, thanks for your call. As you can hear, it sounds like I am sitting in a sawmill! The contractors are putting up a new addition. Please give me 30 seconds as I move to an area free of distractions."
- "Sandy, I'm sorry. This conversation is important, but I'm having trouble hearing with all that noise from the plant. Is there some place quiet we could go to talk?"

Barrier to Listening: Bad Connectivity
Let's face it: As great as it is, mobile technology has its drawbacks. Driving through tunnels, riding in elevators, and other limitations of mobile technology increase your risk of having a bad connection, thereby impacting your ability to hear and to listen. In addition, straining to hear the tinny output of a $39 speakerphone can cause pains in the neck, back, and other places.

Brilliant Practices that address bad connectivity include:
- Buy and operate high-quality equipment.

- Test devices ahead of time to confirm a good signal and sound quality.
- Stay stationary during your conversations.
- Use a landline.
- Schedule calls for times when you are not driving or riding.
- Invest in high-quality headphones. They not only improve sound quality, but they also minimize background interference and unwanted sounds.

Barrier to Listening: Device Distraction
Chiming alerts on your calendar, the Boing! of text messages, and flashing updates on your iPad get in the way of listening.

Brilliant Practice: Turn them off. Make a point of shutting down while in front of the customer. This shows respect and also improves the probability that the customer will do the same.

A Shining Example might sound like this: "Let me power this down...my grandson likes to mess with my ringtones. Who knows what we might hear. Last week it was Homer Simpson singing 'Stairway to Heaven.'"

Barrier to Listening: Multitasking
Any and all attempts at multitasking—feeding your dog or playing *Angry Birds* while on a conference call, responding to instant messages during a meeting, attempting phone conversations while driving—limit your focus.

Brilliant Practice: Don't do it! Move somewhere free of gadgetry and distractions. Get out of traffic and park in a quiet spot.

Here's a good Shining Example to eliminate this barrier to listening: "Charlie, bear with me a minute...I'm pulling off the road to park so I can concentrate on our conversation."

Barrier to Listening: Language Issues
When participants in a conversation share a common first language, they not only share common words, but they also share

the interpretations and nuances typical of that language. However, when participants in a conversation have different first languages, much of that contextual background knowledge does not exist. Words and phrases may be used differently with different meanings, and the potential for misinterpretation skyrockets.

Even when participants share the first language, different geographies have different dialects that impact the meaning of words, how they are pronounced, the speed at which they are spoken, and even the emphasis of the syllables. Winston Churchill observed that Great Britain and the United States were two nations divided by a common language. Spanish spoken in Spain is quite different from the Spanish spoken in Mexico. Have you ever listened in on a conversation with someone from New York City talking to someone from Selma, Alabama? Holy moly!

Furthermore, different age groups, social classes, and professions have their own special jargon. Different industries, and even different companies within industries, have their own dictionary of speech. I remember with horror my first week at Xerox Learning Systems, hearing the thud of a three-inch binder being dropped on my desk, the contents of which defined, in 12-point type, the thousands of Xerox acronyms used within the company. Learning Klingon would probably have been easier.

"That dog don't hunt" will resonate with most folks from the southern United States. "Bob's your uncle" is very clear to those who are versed in 18th century British sailor speak. He is a "rate buster" makes sense to those familiar with manufacturing unions. She is a "nosey parker" is a standard term in South Africa. "First in, first out" is a key term in the accounting world. And then there is "buying a pig in a poke," and on and on.

Often, not wanting to look stupid, most people will not ask the meaning of something if they do not understand it. They will make their best guess and hope/assume they are correct. Here are three Brilliant Practices that address language issues:

- Talk slowly and enunciate clearly. This will encourage the customer to do the same. And when you are unsure of the intended meaning of what the customer said, question to clarify. A Shining Example might be: "Roberta, just to be clear, please explain what you mean by MTBF?"

- Ask the other person to share key points via e-mail. Often, people who don't speak a specific language well will have good reading and writing skills.

    After the third time you have communicated to the customer that you do not understand what he is trying to say, a Shining Example comment would be: "Mr. Customer, I have an idea that might help both of us to make sure we have a common understanding. Would you be kind enough to e-mail me in detail your description of the problem, what you have done to address it so far, the results you have gotten, and your thoughts for getting this problem resolved? Once I receive this, I will get back to you within 24 hours."

- Address the issue head-on. State that jargon and acronyms are real, and ask everyone attending your meeting to bring them to your attention at any time throughout the conversation. This gives people permission and helps them save face.

    Here is a Shining Example of what you might say: "Thank you, Tom, and the rest of your customer team, for meeting with us. Before we move into the agenda, I'd like to make a request. I am not sure about your company, but we use more jargon and acronyms than neurosurgeons at a brain conference! May I please ask everyone to question any term or phrase that you are not exactly sure the meaning of? Thank you...we will do the same."

Barrier to Listening: Cultural Differences

In addition to different first languages and disparate dialects, people from countries other than your own may have distinctive cultures that impact appropriate rules of behavior and styles of communication. Nonverbal communication is often different.

For example, nodding your head up and down may mean yes to you but no to your customer. Silence may signify lack of interest to some, but to those from another country, it may be a sign of respect to a more senior person within their company. Manners and protocol vary, and unless those differences are understood, the quality of communication will suffer. These two Brilliant Practices apply to addressing cultural differences:

- Do your homework. Purchase guides for doing business in other countries. Ask people you know who are experienced in dealing with those cultures.
- Show respect. Let the customer know that you respect them and would never willingly do something to the contrary. If possible, find a coach within the customer organization who can give you some guidance when necessary.

Barrier to Listening: Emotional State of Mind
If you have important issues at home, it can be very difficult to concentrate. The stress of dealing with significant and complex problems compounds the challenges of listening. Short time frames to complete work and multiple requests for your help all add frustration fuel to the fire of stress. Sometimes the customer starts giving you negative feedback that you take personally. When this occurs, the natural tendency is to shut down, get self-protective, and start creating your defense. Like a stray cat trapped in an alley, you will look for ways to either escape or attack—not a good approach to building relationships. Brilliant Practices that are appropriate when your state of mind is less than optimal include:

- Postpone or delay the conversation, if possible.
- Try to compartmentalize. Force yourself to shut out everything else but the current conversation. Take two minutes before your conversation to clear your mind and relax. Remind yourself that the customer is upset about the situation—don't take it personally. Deep breathing works for many people.

Barrier to Listening: Personality Differences

Maybe you're a get-to-the-point, get-'er-done kind of guy and the customer likes to take his time and ramble on. Maybe you prefer the big-picture, blue-ocean way of thinking and the customer likes to count the grains of sand. Maybe your natural tendency is to see the glass as full to the rim and your customer sees the glass as almost empty. When you're not feeling in sync with your customer, remember these Brilliant Practices:

- Tell yourself that slow talking does not necessarily mean slow thinking. Remember that some people speak in paragraphs, not sentences (whereas teenagers speak in grunts).
- Flex your style to match your customer's style. If the customer speaks slowly, consciously slow your speech. If the customer wants to talk specifics, do it.

Barrier to Listening: Your Attitude about the Conversation

You may feel that the conversation is unimportant, unnecessary, a waste of your time, or that you can add little value. These two Brilliant Practices will help provide you with an attitude adjustment toward the conversation at hand:

- Remember the customer feels that the conversation is important—hence, if it is important to the customer, it should be important to you. Focus.
- If the conversation has limited value, don't have it. Review what is needed via e-mail or ask someone else to handle it if you can.

Barrier to Listening: Your Attitude toward the Other Person

Being the very smart, worldly, sophisticated individual that you are, it is easy to let your big ego get in the way. You might feel that the other person is not worthy to be in your presence, let alone have a conversation with you! Maybe you have a lack of respect for the other person based upon past experience or what you think you know about that person. Maybe you just don't like the other person. The Brilliant Practice to remember in these instances is simple: Get over it!

Barrier to Listening: Your Intelligence and Experience
You are an expert with deep knowledge that you want to share, and keeping your lips from moving is about as easy as keeping Old Faithful from spouting off steam. Being experienced, you have the ability to take limited information and jump to conclusions. Much of the time you will be right, but sometimes you will get it all wrong. At the point when you think you have things all figured out, your tendency is to stop listening and focus on next steps. This is a bad idea. From that point on, you start hearing what you want to hear and block out all else. You may start thinking of what you will say next, impatient for the customer to stop talking so that you can demonstrate your magnificence. To keep your radiance in check, consider these Brilliant Practices:

- Don't anticipate the period at the end of a sentence. A conversation is not a sporting event! It may be acceptable to start talking/cheering/yelling during the last few measures of the national anthem at a baseball game, but not during a conversation. Let the other person end her thought, and then pause to make sure she is finished. Count to five before talking, paraphrase the key points you think you heard, and get customer confirmation before speaking.
- Act as if the customer conversation is mission critical. Remember the line and the attitude from the movie *Apollo 13* when attempting to get the astronauts back on earth safely: "Failure is not an option."
- Assume positive intent. Most people want to do well and to do the right thing.
- Believe that everyone you talk to is smart and has a good idea or two that you can learn from.
- Show respect for their foibles and distinct peculiarities.
- When possible, instead of talking over the phone, schedule

the meeting face-to-face.
- Listen with your eyes as well as your ears.

Further, pre-planning is always a great idea. Try engaging these Brilliant Practices before your conversation takes place:
- Prepare and share an agenda ahead of the conversation.
- Plan for notes to be taken (see the sidebar at the end of this chapter).
- If multiple members of your organization are to participate in the conversation, prepare and plan ahead as to roles and responsibilities. Quantify objectives, anticipate customer re-actions, and discuss how to handle objections.
- If you know you may have difficulty understanding the cus-tomer for whatever reason, ask others from your organiza-tion to participate.
- Write out the probes you will ask ahead of time so that you concentrate on what is being said, and not what you will say.
- If possible, take five minutes directly prior to a conversation to relax and mentally prepare. Review the seven trust build-ers. Tell yourself to keep quiet and focus.
  I will share more thoughts on pre-planning in Chapter 7.

To listen with intensity, you need to ask the right questions. Probing with purpose is the key.

Probing with Purpose

Probing helps you gain information in real time directly from the customer. Done effectively, it helps you to take, and keep, control of the conversation and guide the discussion to best help the cus-tomer. It can help reduce customer anxiety by airing any angst as well as clear up fuzzy thinking on either the customer's part or on your part by talking things through in depth. As the customer responds to your questions, it moves them toward cooperation and collaboration. Good questioning allows you to sow your ideas, stimulate thinking, and test possible solutions. Finally, asking well-thought-out, customer-appropriate questions shows your respect of the customer and builds your credibility.

There are two broad categories of probes: open probes and closed probes. Each has a different purpose, like screwdrivers in your toolkit — sometimes a flathead will do, and sometimes you need a Phillips.

Closed Probes

"Ma'am, should I save your child or your dog first?"

A closed probe limits the range of the customer's response to a yes or no, or a choice among selected alternatives. In addition, closed probes should be used when you want to confirm your understanding.

Shining Examples of closed probes that limit customer response are questions such as these:

- "Is downtime a concern?"
- "Which looks best for you, the Silver or the Gold service contract?"
- "Are you interested in validating the results?"
- "Do you want to get started?"
- "Who besides yourself is involved in making this decision?"
- "Does this make sense?"
- "Which approach do you feel is more appropriate?"
- "Does this jacket complement my blue eyes?"
- "Could the salespeople sell it if they had a gun to their heads?"
- "Who owns the process?"
- "We can begin the engagement this month or start in June — which time frame is best for you?"
- "Have you tried to fix this problem before?"

- "Which city would you prefer to hold the workshop in — Barcelona, Spain, or Ottumwa, Iowa?"
- "Has anyone measured the impact of the nonperformance?"
- "Who else would benefit from the change?"
- "Which issue is the more critical — cost or quality?"
- "Is improving quality a nice-to-do or a priority?"

Shining Examples of closed probes that are designed to confirm understanding include:
- "In other words, failure is not an option?"
- "So what you are saying is, the problem only occurs at peak hours?"
- "Let me see if I am on track: Fred loves the idea, Sue is against it, and Tommy just doesn't care. Is that it?"
- "Just to confirm, we have to go live no later than August 6, correct?"
- "Wow, so your job is on the line if this engagement fails?"

Open Probes
"Dr. Einstein, what are the secrets of the universe?"
The open probe has two related purposes. You should ask an open probe when you want to allow the customer to respond freely in order to gain general information or when you want to encourage expansion. Open probes require an in-depth response.

Open probes are powerful. Like an open road, open probes invite exploration. At the same time, they guide the conversation along the path of your purpose and intention. They allow the customer to become actively involved and take ownership of the verbal exchange. Furthermore, they create a conversational tone and eliminate the interrogation style of yes-no responses elicited from a continuous barrage of closed probes. Open probes allow the customer to do what they want to do — talk about something they want to talk about.

Flash Point: You are trying to converse with a colleague, not interrogate a prisoner.

Shining Examples of open probes sound like these:
- "What are your top priorities for the new year?"
- "How will you make your decision?"
- "Under what circumstances does the problem occur?"
- "Personally, what does the success of this project mean to you?"
- "What solutions are you considering?"
- "Why is knowledge management an issue now?"
- "What special considerations are there?"
- "How do you feel about the results from the proof of concept?"
- "To date, what have you done to try to fix this?"
- "How are you dealing with the manpower shortage?"
- "What is your timetable for completion?"
- "What has been your experience with service contracts in the past?"
- "Show me the process steps as they are established now."
- "How do you decide if escalation is needed?"
- "You stated that senior management now sees services as strategic. What prompted this change in attitude?"
- "How does our recommendation align with your thinking?"
- "What will happen to you personally if this is not resolved?"

Sometimes, stimulating comments give the same results as open probes. Statements such as the Shining Examples listed below encourage the customer to provide more information, and thus, they perform the same function as an open probe. Keep them in your toolkit right next to the open probes and use them interchangeably.

- "Say more about that."
- "Tell me what you are looking for."
- "Walk me through your decision process, please."
- "Describe your thinking, please."
- "Please explain the problem."
- "Really?"
- "Oh?"

In addition, sometimes nonverbal actions act as open probes. Questioning actions such as opening up your hands, cocking your head, or putting a quizzical look on your face will prompt further explanation from the customer. Just as a dog's paw on the hand encourages more pets, a look of genuine interest triggers more discussion.

Finally, one of the most powerful ways to get the customer to elaborate is to say nothing. Most people become uncomfortable when silence enters a conversation. Hence, they will fill the communication void and expand more on the topic being discussed.

Flash Point: Silence is your friend.

Problem Solving versus Opportunity Finding
It is very important to note that your "probe of choice" will depend on the situation. When you are in firefighting mode trying to fix a customer problem, closed probes are the most efficient and the most desirable. During a problem-solving discussion, 80 percent or more of the probes you ask should be closed probes. As a proven problem solver, my guess is that you are already very good at this. When problem solving, keep doing what you are doing.

However, when you are in a proactive, opportunity-finding

mode, things are just the opposite. To be effective, 80 percent or more of the probes you ask should be open probes.

Research bears this out. In sales conversations, top sellers asked significantly fewer closed probes than other sellers. By asking more open probes, customers were more actively involved in the conversation, and involvement correlates with success.[1] Hence, anyone trying to influence someone to take action should follow suit; when asking questions, keep most of them open probes.

Now that you know this, you can easily apply this approach to your customer conversations, correct? Wrong. It doesn't work that way. This is not natural behavior. Whatever the profession, a person's natural tendency is to ask mainly closed probes. To repeat, it is desirable to ask primarily closed probes when problem solving. However, when the BSP wants to be proactive, she needs to change her probing behavior, consciously focusing on asking primarily open probes. I'll talk more about this later in both Chapters 5 and 6.

Presenting Powerfully

Flash Point: To earn the right to present your ideas, you must first clearly understand the customer's situation (facts and feelings), and then let the customer know you understand her situation.

Presenting powerfully is all about getting your message across clearly and succinctly, in a manner that the customer understands and accepts. This skill is used to make a recommendation for future action or to share a decision that has already been made. It is made up of three components: the "what," which states the item or direction you are recommending; the "why," which clarifies the reason you feel it is appropriate; and the "benefit," which explains what the customer will gain by following your recommendation.

To better illustrate this concept, here's a Shining Example that is appropriate when making a recommendation:

- What: "What I'd recommend for you is our Platinum contract."
- Why: "Why I think it is appropriate is that it gives you direct access to Tier 3 personnel."
- Benefit: "The benefit is that by having access to our best and brightest, you will get your issues addressed faster and maximize your uptime."

In reality, most people are pretty good about explaining the "what," many are good at telling the "why," but the majority stinks at communicating the benefit; they assume the customer "gets" it. That's a shame, because to the customer, the benefit is the most important thing! (And no, they probably don't get it.)

I strongly recommend that you use the actual words "what," "why," and "benefit" when you present to your customer, for two reasons: The first is that after you get used to doing this, the what-why-benefit rhythm will act as a mantra to help you remember to include all three parts. The second reason is that using these words in a series will act as a guide for the listener that will help him follow your logic path and better understand your intended result.

Here is a Shining Example when presenting a decision to your customer:

- What: "What we did was expand our contract options to offer dedicated support account managers for each geographic region."
- Why: "Why we did this was that select customers like you wanted a single point of contact by area."

- Benefit: "The benefit is that it will make things easier for you while getting problems resolved sooner."

Powerfully Presenting: Your 30-Second Elevator Pitch
Have you ever been at a barbeque, fundraiser, or public seminar, when the person next to you says, "Just what do you do, anyway?" I remember the first time this happened to me, and I was totally unprepared for the question! My response included a portion of hemming and hawing, a side dish of umms and ahhs, and a main course of incoherent blabber. Not my finest presentation!

The truth is that at some point, a customer executive or other very important person will ask you this question. And you will have less than a minute to give a professional response — one that clearly defines what you do, why you do it, and the benefit it brings the person you are talking to.

If this hasn't happened yet, believe me, it will. I also guarantee that unless you are prepared, you and the other person will be very disappointed in your response. Hence, prepare, practice, and be ready. The good news is that you already know how to do it — just use the skill of presenting powerfully.

Scenario: You are on site working at a customer location. As you enter the elevator on the 12th floor, the customer Big Boss gets on, notices the logo and title on your briefcase tag, and says, "What does a service professional for Big Boppers do, anyway?"

Here is an exercise that will help you develop your 30-second elevator pitch:
1. Write out how you will respond appropriately within the 30 seconds you have before the door opens in the lobby, including what you do, why it is important, and the benefits to the Big Boss.
2. Present your response out loud.
3. Critique your response using the following quality criteria:
   - Relevant: The presentation addressed the topics, issues, needs, and requirements of interest to the Big Boss.

- Clear: The presentation was free of jargon, used simple words and familiar language to convey the message, and umms, ahhs, and other unnecessary terms were avoided.
- Succinct: All key points of the presentation were given in a logical way within the allotted time.
- Accurate: All information shared was correct.
- Persuasive: The presentation showed the Big Boss how you deliver value via the what-why-benefit.
- Polished: Your preparation and practice showed through in a confident, professional manner.

4. Edit your response as necessary. Get comfortable with your response by practicing. Edit and practice, edit and practice….

Here's a Shining Example of a 30-second elevator pitch:
Slipping through the closing door of the elevator, the customer Big Boss glances at you and says: "Just what do you do, anyway?"

Brilliant Service Professional: "Mr. Bellamy, isn't it? I recognized you from your picture in your company's annual report. I am Sammy Sampson, your service account manager from Big Boppers, the company that provides the software that makes your network tick like a Swiss watch. Thank you for being a great customer.

"What I do is act as a single source of contact for your company for all things network. I work with Samuel Barrow, your CIO, and his team, along with my network experts from Big Boppers.

"Why I do this is so that when there is a problem, we fix it fast, and better yet, we focus on keeping problems from occurring. I'm pleased to say that you enjoy a 99.6 percent uptime.

"The benefit to you is that you can rest assured that your customers will be able to smoothly make their purchases online during this busy holiday season and thus provide profitable revenue to help you accomplish your business goals.

"Here is my card. It was a pleasure meeting you."

Wow! Wasn't that smooth? It is amazing the positive impression you can make when you are prepared.

Acknowledging Concerns

Addressing concerns is an ongoing part of the BSP's job. Every customer will have concerns with you, or your offerings, or your company, or just the situation the customer finds herself in from time to time. You should anticipate and welcome concerns, because when you deal with them quickly and effectively, you build credibility and trust.[2]

As Figure 4.1 displays, when customers work with you, their emotions can vary greatly, depending upon the situation. Often they are accepting or open, and sometimes they are interested in or excited about what you are doing or what you are suggesting. However, sometimes customer circumstances trigger concerns — concerns that range from being skeptical, such as doubting what they have been told, to being annoyed that call backs take too long, to being irritated because they have been told different things by different people in your company, to being angry because their problems are taking weeks to be addressed. In ex-

Figure 4.1

The Customer Emotion Meter

1	2	3	4	5	6	7	8	9	10
Excited	Interested	Positive	Open	Accepting	Skeptical	Annoyed	Irritated	Angry	Raging

treme cases, they may express rage caused by desperation or fear that the situation they face is out of control.

Whether supported by facts or conjured up in their imagination, these concerns are certainly real to the customer at that time. To earn the right to address the facts and the underlying root cause, the BSP must first address the feelings by acknowledging the customer's concern.

The words you use are very important, so thoughtfully consider what you will say using the guide I'll introduce shortly. But the old saying, "It is not just what you say, but how you say it," shines with truth. This is especially important when dealing with anxiety or resistance. Consciously slowing your pace will be seen as caring. Lowering your voice adds assurance. Actions such as maintaining eye contact, leaning forward, and opening up your hands nonverbally confirms that you understand the importance the customer is conveying.

> Flash Point: When acknowledging concerns, talk slow and talk low.

There are four steps you must follow to address and resolve customer concerns:

1. **Remain calm.** Professionals remain calm under pressure. This immediately lowers tension.

2. **Pause before responding.** This is a sign of respect that also calms the customer. Another benefit of pausing is that it gives you the chance to think, especially if your initial reaction is, *Holy smokes! Where did that come from?*

3. **Demonstrate empathy.** When the customer feels that you understand her situation or her opinion and she knows you care about how she feels, tension is removed from the conversation. Once the feelings are addressed, the customer is ready

to deal with the facts. You should demonstrate empathy anytime you sense negativity, as it will immediately help calm the customer and open the door to deeper understanding.

4. **Indicate what you plan to do about it.** Often, using the what-why-benefit approach to recommend a plan of action is a good way to respond, followed by a closed probe to confirm that the customer agrees.

Flash Point: Do not even think about problem solving until the four steps of acknowledging concerns have been successfully completed.

Here's a Shining Example I call "Big Trouble on Flight 407":

1. Remain calm (airline pilot in low, modulated voice): "Good afternoon, Ladies and Gentlemen, and thank you for flying Big Sky. Those of you on the right-hand side of the aircraft may have already noticed that the starboard engine is on fire."

2. Pause before responding.

3. Demonstrate empathy: "If I were sitting back there, I'd naturally be concerned, wondering what is going to happen."

4. Indicate what you plan to do about it: "My co-pilot and I have a combined 40 years of experience. During this time, we have been in challenging situations similar to this one and have always had a safe outcome. What we are doing is consulting with our company experts, discussing our options. Why we are taking this approach is to make certain that we determine the best course of action. The benefit is that we are extremely confident that we all will be safely on the ground shortly. Feel free to use your cell phones, but I'd encourage you to remain calm so as not to alarm your loved ones — we will all be fine. I will be back to you shortly with an update."

A high-anxiety situation? Absolutely! But compare the probable reaction to the above scenario if the captain had shouted, "We are all going to die!"

The Challenge of Being Experienced and Really Smart

An expert has a high level of confidence that if he can just get the facts, he can fix the problem. In fact, his career and personal pride may be directly related to this. Therefore, acknowledging concerns is a skill that does not come naturally to many expert problem solvers.

In fact, the natural tendency of a proven problem solver is to skip all four of the steps to acknowledging concerns and immediately try to fix the problem, running roughshod over the customer's feelings like a bulldozer in a meadow. Many times the customer will tolerate your brash approach and acquiesce to your inquisition just to get their issue addressed, but they will not appreciate your total lack of respect for their feelings. You don't build trust with a sledgehammer.

Here is a somewhat extreme example that demonstrates this potential problem:

Angry Customer: "The stainless-steel blade on your mixer flew off and hit my Old Blue's leg!"

Lousy Service Provider: "Huh, never heard that one before. What model number is it?"

Really Angry Customer: "Didn't you hear what I said? Your piece-of-junk product almost killed my champion show dog!"

Lousy Service Provider: "It's not a piece of junk. You probably didn't operate it correctly."

Raging Customer: "Listen, buddy, I want your name now, and I want the name and phone number of your boss, your boss's boss, and your boss's boss's boss! No, better yet, give me your address, you loser! I am going to drive across town and punch you in the face! Then I am posting the truth about you and your company in my blog, on the Losers.com website, and on Facebook,

Google+, and LinkedIn. I may even take out an ad in *The Wall Street Journal* and *The New York Times*! I won't rest until you and your company are publicly shamed, your stock price tumbles, and you are at the train station playing a harmonica for tips!"

Now this may be a slight exaggeration, but you get the drift. There is always a downside of not fixing the customer first, and sometimes that downside can be really big. Hence, you should remain calm, pause before responding, and demonstrate empathy anytime you sense concern, skepticism, annoyance, irritation, anger, or rage, as it will immediately help calm the customer and open the door to deeper understanding.

Below are more Shining Examples of acknowledging concerns in typical service scenarios.

Skeptical Customer: "I have zero confidence in these reports! This information cannot be right."

Brilliant Service Professional:
1. Remain calm.
2. Pause before responding.
3. Demonstrate empathy: "I appreciate your concern about getting accurate reports. You need them to manage your department effectively."
4. Indicate what you plan to do about it: "I'd like to take a few minutes to review some of your data. Do you have a quiet area where I can work until I find the cause?"

Annoyed Customer: "Your website won't accept my password."

Brilliant Service Professional:
1. Remain calm.
2. Pause before responding.
3. Demonstrate empathy: "I get annoyed when that happens to me."
4. Indicate what you plan to do about it: "Let me ask you a couple of questions so that we can get you into the system."

Annoyed Customer: "This is not nearly as simple as your salesperson said it would be!"

Brilliant Service Professional:

1. Remain calm.
2. Pause before responding.
3. Demonstrate empathy: "I understand it takes a while to get comfortable operating a new machine, especially with a new procedure to follow."
4. Indicate what you plan to do about it: "If your time permits, I'd like to walk you through the first important operations step by step."

Irritated Customer: "I was told the consumables would be here last Friday."

Brilliant Service Professional:

1. Remain calm.
2. Pause before responding.
3. Demonstrate empathy: "I can understand how frustrating the delay might be."
4. Indicate what you plan to do about it: "I am checking the status right now, and then we can discuss options for getting this shipment quickly and avoiding problems in the future."

Irritated Customer: "May 30 is not fast enough. I need that software in place by the end of March."

Brilliant Service Professional:

1. Remain calm.
2. Pause before responding.
3. Demonstrate empathy: "I can certainly see why you want the software implementation as soon as possible. Sounds like it is critical to the business."
4. Indicate what you plan to do about it: "I'd like to do some research and get back to you by this Thursday with some possible options to move things up. Is that OK?"

Irritated Customer: "You are the fourth person I have been transferred to! I am really getting irritated!"

Brilliant Service Professional:

1. Remain calm.
2. Pause before responding.
3. Demonstrate empathy: "If I were you, I'd feel exactly the same way. I know being switched from person to person can be frustrating. I will do my best to make this your last transfer."
4. Indicate what you plan to do about it: "Let me ask you a couple of questions, please, and see if we can get this resolved for you."

There are times when the customer is in such a heightened state of hysteria that one pass is not enough. In these cases, you need to repeat steps 1 through 3 again…and maybe again. I call this lather-rinse-repeat. How long do you continue? Until the customer has finally calmed down, gets worn out, or becomes embarrassed. Here's an example of how this might play out.

Angry Customer: "Your company sent me the wrong part three times in a row!"

Brilliant Service Professional:

1. Remain calm.
2. Pause before responding.
3. Demonstrate empathy: "Wow, I know that's really frustrating."

Customer: "Yes, it is frustrating. Why must I waste my time on something that should be so simple?"

Brilliant Service Professional:

1. Remain calm.
2. Pause before responding.
3. Demonstrate empathy: "I hear you loud and clear, and yes, it should be simple."

Customer: "Three times in a row…do you keep tally? Is that a record?"

Brilliant Service Professional:

1. Remain calm.
2. Pause before responding.
3. Demonstrate empathy: "Three times in a row is twice too many. I can imagine how I would feel."

Customer (sounding embarrassed): "Oh, I know it isn't your fault. Sorry for unloading on you."

Brilliant Service Professional:

1. Remain calm.
2. Pause before responding.
3. Demonstrate empathy: "I understand."
4. Indicate what you plan to do about it: "I'd like to gather some information now so we can get you the right part."

More Brilliant Practices to keep in mind are:

- It is not appropriate to jump directly to problem-solving mode until the customer feels acknowledged — fix the customer first.
- Low and slow is the way to go. When you lower your voice and talk more slowly than normal, it often helps to calm the customer.
- Remember the power of your nonverbal behavior. When your body language communicates that you care, the actual words you use are secondary.

Apply the four core relationship skills as described, and you will have the skills to flawlessly do your job right the first time, which is the topic of the next chapter.

Brilliant Practice: Taking Notes

Having accurate notes of a conversation can greatly improve the quality of follow-up and minimize potential errors. Here are a few proven ways to do it:

1. Have an experienced professional take notes of the conversation. This is ideal. Years ago, my secretary would sit in on meetings and use her shorthand skills to accurately record the conversation, freeing me to concentrate on the other person.

2. If you have team members on the call, designate one person skilled in taking notes to act in that role. Again, this will free you up to focus on the other person, what is being said, and how it is being said.

3. Record the conversation. In the right situation, recording the conversation (with permission) is the best way to go. For example, when doing customer research, I ask interviewers to record the conversations and not take notes. This is a quality-control measure that minimizes misinterpretation and captures the actual words of the customer.

4. Take your own notes. This sounds like multitasking, I know, but bear with me. Here is an example that works well for me when I don't have someone else tasked with taking notes: "Mr. Customer, this is an important conversation, and I want to make sure I have full understanding. Do you mind if I take notes?" (This is a sign of respect, and of course the customer will say yes. By making this commitment, you will listen more intensely because you are a professional and do not want to look stupid in the eyes of your customer.) "Thank you. I will commit to getting them to you by noon on Tuesday." (This sets the

stage for you to show your reliability.) "Does that sound OK? All I would ask, though, is that you review my notes and look for anything I missed or anything I got wrong. Fair enough? Maybe you could send your response to me by Thursday at noon?" (The customer is now committed to listen with intensity. He does not want to look stupid either, so he will focus more on the conversation as well.)

Taking accurate notes while actively leading a conversation is a skill that not many (if any) people can do well, hence the beauty of having someone else (in this case, your customer) focused on it. And my feeling is that taking mediocre notes is better than having no notes at all.

Therefore, I suggest this approach: Don't try to record each and every detail; focus intently on the conversation and only jot down key points. However, set aside time to sit down immediately after the conversation and write down everything you remember. If you had established an agenda before the conversation, it will make this much easier. If you are rushed, use your phone to dictate what you remember. Allow time to revisit what you have put down to get the best accuracy you can. Then, at 11:57 a.m. on Tuesday send an e-mail to the customer that says: "Mr. Customer, it was great talking with you last week. On a personal note, I am so glad to hear that your daughter's wedding went well! As promised, here are my notes from our conversation. I'm looking forward to your feedback. Also, after mulling things over, I included two suggestions as to how we might want to move forward. Thank you, Alex."

CHAPTER 5

Doing It Right the First Time

The Five Steps of
Engagement Management

In this chapter, I introduce the five steps of engagement management that every service professional should follow. Of course, the specific actions are different for an implementation consultant, service account manager, or a support engineer, but the five steps remain the same. I will explain why the easiest way is seldom the best way. As usual, Brilliant Practices and Shining Examples will be provided.

As Figure 5.1 shows, engagement management for a service professional includes five steps:

Figure 5.1

The Five Steps of Engagement Management

Plan Ahead	Fix the Customer	Fix the Product	Communicate the Value	Explore Opportunities

1. **Plan Ahead.** Proactively prepare to improve the probability of doing the service job right the first time ("do it right the first time," or DIRTFT).
2. **Fix the Customer.** Inform the customer of your intended actions, setting expectations and addressing concerns.
3. **Fix the Product.** Use your technical skills to repair the product or perform the service (install, implement, maintain, update, or assess).
4. **Communicate the Value.** Let the customer know what you did, why you did it, and the benefit to him.
5. **Explore Opportunities.** When appropriate, discuss and make recommendations to improve the customer's future success.

Step 1: Plan Ahead

Many of the obstacles that stand in the way of doing the job right the first time are a result of failing to plan ahead.

Furthermore, the smarter and more experienced you are, the more tempting it is to just "wing it," relying on your stellar intellectual prowess and vast experience to make the right call on the spot. Beware of this extreme confidence (a.k.a. cockiness). The very best, out-of-this-world service professionals always plan ahead. There is no astronaut, on or off of this planet, who does not rely on checklists and other tools to plan ahead prior to every mission.

Planning ahead embraces the proactive concept integral to the value-creating mindset required of the BSP. Whether it's the support engineer reviewing active cases and contemplating the probable incoming calls to the help desk, the FSE checking his van for parts and consumables inventory for upcoming customer visits, the SAM thinking through what to present at an upcoming quarterly business review, or the technical consultant reviewing the project plan for a software implementation, planning ahead improves the probability of DIRTFT, whatever the service task.

Flash Point: Planning ahead saves time. Often a few minutes spent pondering and preparing saves hours of floundering and failing.

There are three actions to planning ahead — investigate, anticipate, and contemplate — as described below.

Action 1: Investigate

As the service pro prepares for the day or for a specific call, the first action is to investigate — to tap into the relevant knowledge that she and her colleagues and her company have already acquired on that customer.

Assuming that you are technically competent, this collected knowledge is the prime driver of your task of making your customer successful. To make this knowledge productive, you must assimilate and integrate the information relevant to your task to help you consider courses of action and make decisions as to how to proceed. At one extreme, your knowledge source could rely solely on what you remember (not a good idea for gray-hairs like me!). If the products, services, and situations you deal with are very simple, you might be able to get by using this approach, at least until your little gray cells really turn gray.

However, for most of us, business life is much more complex and has far too many moving parts to be able to rely on your personal memory alone. You need a knowledge management system (KMS) to broaden, deepen, and enrich what is already between your ears, to act as a tool to make better decisions easier and faster. A KMS is a formal, systematic process to help create, store, and disperse an organization's expertise. A solid KMS con-

sists of the following information and tools:
- **Product knowledge.** For each product, data sheets and manuals that outline technical requirements and performance specifications are a must. Service bulletins that highlight product issues and recommended steps to address them are a requirement. Lessons learned from your service colleagues on how to do specific work easier, better, and faster can be a huge benefit as well.
- **Customer knowledge.** A customer history that provides product purchases, their application and usage, warranty status, and a log of customer contacts including issues, actions taken, outcomes, and status are invaluable. The type and details of the service contracts in place for what products and at what locations is another must.

This information may be contained in a formal software system, Excel spreadsheets, notebooks, or an assortment of napkins with notes you have assembled while eating at your favorite diner. What is most important is that the information contained is accurate, thorough, and appropriate. It is a huge plus, or course, if this data is easy to access (anywhere, anytime) and easy to use.

Along with the documents listed above, an address book with the numbers of smart, experienced people within your company who are willing to share their expertise can be a huge benefit. In fact, if your formal document-centered KMS is weak, I recommend starting with this approach.

Ideally, your company has a robust KMS in place. However, if it does not, take personal responsibility to gather and develop the information you need. The KMS is the most important tool the service professional can possess.

After you have done your homework and investigated all the readily available information sources in your KMS, it is time for the second action.

Action 2: Anticipate

The next action is to anticipate—to think through possible and probable events. As a service professional, you know that products break, things change, stuff happens. However, when you analyze your personal experiences and the information within your KMS, you are able to anticipate probable issues and potential opportunities. Thinking things through helps you determine what it takes to solve a technical problem, as well as the things that can hinder or stop customer success. As you recall in the section on Potholes on the Path to Perfect Performance in Chapter 1, many things can negatively impact your ability to get the service job done. Considering the most probable problems is time well spent.

Remember also that all customer issues involve feelings as well as facts. Based upon the situation and what you know about the customer, you can anticipate the customer reaction and consider what type of emotion you might have to deal with.

If enough information is available, you move beyond anticipation to prediction, knowing with some degree of certainty that if "X" keeps happening, "Y" will follow. For example, if for some reason your customer has purchased equipment that, at best, will only do a marginal job of meeting his expectations, you can forecast that within a short period of time (say, a couple of weeks), someone in your company will get a call from this customer complaining about the lack of performance of your machine. You can also predict, with a high level of accuracy, that the emotional pot of negativity is simmering on the customer stove, with the potential to boil over if the heat is not turned down.

Action 3: Contemplate

Upon completing Actions 1 and 2, it is now time to contemplate possible next steps. Here you think through possible options and the pluses and minuses of each one. Here are example questions you might ask yourself as you contemplate a specific customer situation: Is this issue mission critical, important, or a nice-to-do from the customer's perspective? What options might work? What are the pluses and minuses of each option (e.g., quality, time, budget, hassle) to the customer, sales, my company, and me? What is the impact if the customer escalates this up the food chain? What might we do to eliminate, or at least minimize, the impact of anticipated problems? How can I make the customer look good? Will the customer be open to my recommendations, or should I anticipate some resistance? What questions make sense to ask? What is the best way to present my suggestions to the customer?

In the example of the marginal equipment I described in Action 2, as you contemplate the different ways of addressing the issue, you might determine that giving your manager and the sales guy a heads-up call to alert them of the pending problem is a wise idea.

The last, but very important, aspect of contemplating is to visualize your success — picture in your mind a very positive outcome to the call (e.g., the machine up and running with the customer smiling, or you accepting your company's Star Performer award at the annual conference in Rio de Janeiro). Doing so will help relax and calm you, making you more receptive to listening and practicing the seven trust builders, when the time comes.

Step 2: Fix the Customer

For some service professionals, communicating with the customer is about as much fun as swimming in a shark tank. If they had their choice, they'd sneak in, do their service job, and sneak off like a jewel thief at a dinner party. This approach is even more tempting when things are not going well. Who wants grief?

When this urge to hide and sneak strikes, fight it! Bypassing this action of engaging with the key person can result in miscommunication, wasted time, and added expense. It can also lessen your customer's perception of you as a professional. So contact the customer immediately in order to ease anxiety prior to performing any service task. When on site, locate the key person first, look her in the eye, smile, and shake her hand firmly. Act as the credible professional you are.

As was demonstrated in Chapter 4, in the section on acknowledging concerns, it is fruitless to try to address any product issues until the customer knows you understand his situation and that you care about his personal well-being. By now you are well versed in using the four steps to addressing concerns. In addition to the normal concerns associated with problem products, in situations where a customer has an issue that is scheduled to be addressed in the future, the waiting period often hatches the egg of skepticism, which grows anxiety. Hence, the earlier you relieve his anxiety, the more positive the customer will be.

For example, imagine that you have invested several thousand dollars in what you hope will be an awesome home theater system—one that will give you bragging rights with all of your buddies. After several weeks of trying to install it yourself, the system is not working up to par. You admit defeat and call the local electronics shop where you bought the system and set up an appointment for them to come out and fix it.

If you are like me, immediately after I hang up the phone, anxiety kicks in. My self-talk may go something like this: *I wonder if the guy they send knows more than I do, or if he is just some wet-nosed rookie getting trained on my dollar. I hope they don't try and sell me something I don't need. Will he show up on time, or am I going to have to sit and do crossword puzzles for four hours? I am having all of our friends over for the big playoff game Saturday afternoon — will he get it installed in one visit, or won't he? Maybe I should have spent more time looking at other choices. What if the reason I haven't gotten it to work is that I missed something really simple? Then I'll look stupid and still have to pay the bill.*

In some cases, depending on my sleep level, workload, or caffeine consumption, a mild paranoia might set in: *What if they break something or make things worse? Might they be casing my place for a future burglary?* Or worse yet, *I hope he doesn't tell my wife what this system really costs!*

The savvy BSP home theater technician has anticipated my possible emotions while he was planning for my installation. He might head off my negativity with this Shining Example phone call: "Mr. Alexander, I am Robert Bonanza, the senior technician with Gonzo Electronics. I wanted to let you know that I will be at your home as scheduled next Friday between 3:45 p.m. and 4 p.m. to install your home theater system. I understand that you are a best-selling author, noted services pundit, and just an amazing guy! Looking forward to meeting you. I've done several dozen installations similar to yours and look forward to having you enjoying your system within a couple of hours. I've reviewed the notes of your conversation with Maria, our salesperson, and have a good feel for what you want. However, I'd appreciate a few minutes of your time when I first arrive to review your expectations and discuss any issues. Please call me on my cell phone at 231-555-1234 if you have questions. Thank you."

To me, that well-planned, proactive, professional approach would build technician credibility in my mind, reduce my anxiety, and reinforce that I made a good choice in choosing Gonzo. My attitude toward the call might well transition from dread to excitement. How about you? (Note: I added the part about the best-selling author just for fun, but believe me, it would get my attention!)

When the home theater tech arrives, along with acknowledging any concerns I might voice, he has a few more things to accomplish before tackling the technical issues. If it is a product problem, he should start by learning/understanding the symptoms, hearing my objectives, and determining what I have done to try to fix things myself.

The technician might continue "fixing" me, the customer, by saying the following upon his arrival at my home: "Great to meet you. I'm confident we will get you up and running before I leave. I'll start soon by doing an assessment of where things are, to determine what needs to be done. To begin with, though, I'd like to learn more about your home theater objectives, what you see as the problem, and what you have done to address this yourself."

At this point, I am more than happy to provide him with everything he needs.

Here is another Shining Example that applies to fixing the customer:

(Phone call or voicemail): "Mr. Collins, I'm Marko, your FSE from Big Iron. I am scheduled to come to your Bronson facility to fix your 1492 Wampum Converter, a unit I am very familiar with. My plan is to arrive this afternoon between 2:30 p.m. and 4:30 p.m. I'd like to talk with you briefly upon my arrival to make sure that I understand your perspective. If that time works for you, I will call you from the lobby when I arrive. In the interim, please call or text me at 321-555-9876 if you have any questions. Thank you."

This lets the customer know that things are going as planned, that the FSE probably is well qualified, and that the customer has a say in what and how things are done.

Marko may have hoped that when he met Mr. Collins, he would start the conversation by saying something like, "My information indicates that your Wampum converter is down. Does that mean it is not working at all, or not performing to your requirements? What are your expectations? Please tell me what is happening or not happening. What have you done to try to fix it? Has anything else occurred that might have influenced the situation?"

However, in preparing for the call, Marko learned that the

customer has been down for a long time. He, therefore, would anticipate negativity and be prepared with a Shining Example that sounds like this:

Customer: "It's about time someone came out here! We've been waiting four days!"

BSP: "I know, and that is four days too many. However, I am here now and will do my best to get you up and running. May I ask you a few short questions to get me going in the right direction? The problem that was communicated to me was that after

---

The Easy Way Is Often Not the Best Way

The support engineer may pick up the phone and hear a customer say: "My X11 is not working. Please send someone to fix it."

The tempting response, especially when there are 96 callers in the queue, might be: "Sure, I will have dispatch schedule someone and they will call you." Yes, the problem is off your plate (at least for now), however, this is seldom the appropriate response.

Instead, here is a Shining Example of how to address this situation: Customer: "My X11 is not working. Please send out someone to fix it."

BSP: "I am sorry to hear that. Of course we will help you get your X11 up and running. What I suggest is that I ask you a few select questions. Why I recommend this is because it will help me determine how to provide the most appropriate service. The benefit will be getting you up and running as quickly as possible. Is that OK with you? Now tell me, what is the machine not doing that you want it to do?"

running continuously for eight hours, it just quit…is that correct? Is there anything else I should know? What I'd like to do is run a short diagnostic. Why I suggest this approach is that within just a few minutes it will confirm or disconfirm what we suspect to be the problem. The benefit is that spending 30 minutes up front could save us hours, thereby getting the machine up and producing again as quickly as possible. Does that sound OK to you? Of course, if I find something unexpected I will notify you ASAP. Thank you. I will get back to you as soon as I resolve the problem."

In this scenario, Marko let the customer know he cared as he calmly acknowledged the customer concern; he then asked permission to get down to business. Once he gathered enough information through probing and listening, he presented the what-why-benefit of his planned actions, with the promise of personally reporting the results when the job was completed.

Another Shining Example might look like this:

BSP: "George, I wanted to let you know that I received the notice that you have initiated a Priority 2 escalation. What I will do is take the lead inside my organization in handling this issue. Why I am doing this is to keep things as simple as possible. The benefit of doing this is to make sure we deploy the right resources in the right way to take care of the problem quickly. I will e-mail you between 4 p.m. and 5 p.m. this afternoon to give you a status update. Please contact me anytime you wish."

This lets the customer know that someone owns the issue and has committed to keeping the customer informed. This relieves anxiety. Sometimes, however, you have no information readily available and no time to find it. In most cases, it is best to first proceed to contact the customer to lower anxiety, and then start the problem-solving process. In this case you might say something along these lines: "Ms. Smith, I am Sharon from Dubious Software. I was told to drop everything and call you immediately. I'm sorry, but I have little other information. Please tell me, what is the issue?"

Fixing the customer isn't always about reacting to a product problem. The same steps should be put in place when doing something proactive, such as performing preventive maintenance or conducting an assessment with the goal of improving future performance.

> Flash Point: Even things perceived as positive can cause anxiety—always fix the customer.

Step 3: Fix the Product

In Step Two we fixed the customer. Now it is time to fix the product or implement the service. I won't dwell here, as you have this technical aspect of the job down cold.

Step 4: Communicate the Value

It is now time to present the what-why-benefit of the actions you have taken. Assuming that you were able to fix the product or perform the service appropriately (e.g., fix the machine, install the software, perform preventive maintenance, complete the assessment), it is time to tell the key person what you did, why you did it, and the benefit to that person using language appropriate to the customer. (If you were unable to fix the machine, see Delivering Bad News later in this chapter.)

Here are three great Shining Examples that communicate value to the customer:

- "Mr. Customer, as promised, here is a status report. What I did was dedicate one of our best engineers, Angela, to take the technical lead. Why I chose her is that she is not only sharp, but fast. She has already started a network diagnostic and will have her preliminary data by 7 a.m. tomorrow. She will review the data, confirm issues, and if she is able to identify the root cause, we will get back to you with recommendations. I will e-mail you again tomorrow morning at 10 a.m. to give you an update. The benefit to you is that we are moving quickly to resolution."

This approach demonstrates reliability and helps provide assurance to the customer that the correct actions are being implemented. It also lessens the chance that the customer gets an itchy finger and starts "disaster dialing" — calling every executive in your company and pestering them to get involved to fix the problem.

- "Good Morning, Mr. Customer. As promised, here is the status of the integration project. The details are attached, but overall what we have accomplished this last week is to complete Phase I one week early. Why we were able to accomplish this is that Karen and Bart from your team got up to speed much more quickly than anticipated. Plus, Tony figured out a way to synch both systems in two fewer days. The benefit is that if your management requests a status update, you are going to look very good!"

- "Mr. Customer, I'm pleased to say that our diagnosis was correct. What I did was change the faulty part, clean the capathulum, recalibrate all settings, and update the software. Why I recalibrated the settings was to confirm that everything else is up to standards. The benefit of doing this is that it will ensure uptime and give you a greater return on investment."

A few other "housekeeping" activities need to take place. These include responding to questions, completing the necessary paperwork, providing recommended actions for the customer to follow, and, if necessary, delivering any bad news.

Respond to Questions

Once you have presented the what-why-benefit, it is time to ask the customer if he has any questions. This ensures understanding and invites the customer to become more involved, if she chooses.

Complete Paperwork

If paperwork is required that the customer must sign, now is the time to do it. For example, "Your cost is $350 for the call, and $749 for the part. I will need you to sign here, please."

Recommend Actions

When the service job is completed, it is appropriate to pass along suggestions or tips to improve performance. Here are three Shining Examples:

- Brilliant service pro (talking to the machine operator): "See this doodad here? When that gets dirty, it can sometimes skew the cut. If you just take a rag and wipe it like this a couple of times each day, it can keep things working right and make your job easier. Do you have any questions of me while I am here?"
- Brilliant service pro (talking to the department manager): "Always feel free to call any person in our organization you wish. However, since anyone you contact about your account will pass the ball on to me, you can save time by texting or e-mailing me directly."
- Brilliant service pro (talking to the IT director): "I'm glad I was able to answer your questions. Feel free to contact me anytime. However, in most cases there is a much faster way to get the information you need. May I show you your Key Customer Knowledgebase and an easy way to access what you need?"

Delivering Bad News

Sometimes, no matter how well we plan or how skillful we are, the service job does not get completed as we'd hoped (see Potholes on the Path to Perfect Performance in Chapter 1 for reminders). Do not flee the crime scene! No matter who or what is at fault, you are the designated deliverer of news the customer doesn't want to hear. Instead of presenting the what-why-benefit of what we have done, we now must modify the model. Now, you must explain what has occurred, why it has occurred, and the impact to the customer. Here is the model for delivering bad news:

1. **State the bad news.** "Mr. Customer, what I have to report is bad news. Why it is negative is that although I followed the standard procedures I shared earlier and successfully replaced the defective chip that we both suspected, I also discovered a bad relay that is critical to functionality, and that part is not readily available. The impact is that you will not be up and running until that part can be installed."

   Customer: "I need that machine fixed now!"

2. **Acknowledge the customer's concern.** Remain calm, pause, and demonstrate empathy: "Harry, I know where you are coming from. If I were in your shoes, I'd want the machine repaired immediately."

3. **Provide an explanation.** "Unfortunately, I cannot change the laws of physics. I have checked all sources, and the relay we need is 2,000 miles away. The quickest we can get it here is tomorrow at 8 a.m., if we order it within the next two hours."

4. **Present alternatives.** "Unfortunately, I am booked all day tomorrow at another customer site. However, I could be here first thing Thursday. Or, I have another idea...the fix is straightforward, and your man Freddy has a good understanding of the equipment. What I can do is schedule one of our support engineers to talk Freddy through the process. Why this is a good idea is because it is the fastest way to get you up and running. The benefit is that you will gain one full day of uptime. Can you think of any other options? Which would you prefer?"

Customer: "I don't like either choice. I need that equipment up now!"

Lather, rinse, repeat until the customer is in "acceptance mode."

5. **Get the customer to buy in.** "I hear you, Harry, but I don't see any other possibilities. What do you prefer?"

Customer: "All right. Let's see if Freddy can do it."

6. **Thank the customer.** "Thanks, Harry, I appreciate your understanding, and I appreciate your business. I will set up a support engineer to contact Freddy as soon as I depart."

In the above scenario, the BSP's goals are to: (1) develop the best solution under the circumstances, and (2) calm the customer down by taking him from angry to accepting. Obviously, in this situation, looking for future opportunities would not be appropriate.

Step 5: Explore Opportunities

Exploring opportunities is the process of collaborating with the customer to uncover possible actions that you can take that could improve the customer's situation. Step 5 is often a natural follow-on after a successful Step 4, as the customer is probably pleased with you and the results you achieved. Exploring opportunities is appropriate anytime the customer is open to new ideas.

However, exploring opportunities is not appropriate when the customer has concerns—if the customer is not "fixed" in the present, she will not react kindly to discussions about the future. As was modeled above in Delivering Bad News, do your best to get the customer to accept the situation and wait for another time to explore opportunities.

When the customer is in a positive mood, make recommendations to improve his situation using the what-why-benefit model. For example, you might recommend the customer purchase a service contract in which preventive maintenance might reduce the need for emergency service calls, saving money and maximizing uptime.

In this situation, a Shining Example would be: "What I'd suggest is that you consider signing up for our service contract. Why I think it is a good idea for you is that your machines get a lot of usage, and like all complex pieces of equipment, they will break now and then. The benefits of being under a service contract are that you get priority response, service calls are free, and you get a 20 percent reduction in spare parts—all saving you money. For example, instead of paying the $1,099 for today, you would have paid just $650. If you sign up today, I am authorized to wave my service call. What do you think?"

Well-thought-out engagement management lays out the most effective and most efficient process for working with customers, greatly improving the probability of doing it right the first time. And when that occurs, customers are much more open to exploring opportunities. In the next chapter, we expand upon this theme, discussing how we can influence with integrity to make our customers more successful.

CHAPTER 6

Influencing with Integrity

For the BSP to be the most effective in helping customers be successful, he must rely on persuasion—influencing with integrity.

In this chapter, I build upon the "explore opportunities" step of engagement management discussed in the last chapter. I validate that all professionals rely on influencing to be successful. In fact, they spend almost one-half of their time trying to move others to take action. Services professionals are no exception.

Next, I demonstrate why "selling" does not have to be evil and I point out the differences between selling manipulation and selling with integrity. From there, I outline services management's changing expectations of service professionals in helping the company get new business. This showcases why selling is such an integral part of the BSP role.

You will learn about the customer decision triangle and the connection among technical needs, business issues, and personal wins that are needed to build confidence and urgency with the customer. You'll also be introduced to the Stakeholder Analysis tool. Learning how to use it will enable you to determine the best approach to use with different customers. In addition, I introduce a qualifying tool and a probing model designed to help you prepare for influencing conversations. Finally, I discuss the "teeter-totter" formula for creating value. Of course, I'll share more Brilliant Practices and Shining Examples that will help you apply this content to your everyday reality.

Everyone Is Involved in Non-Sales Selling

Most professionals in all fields spend a sizable portion of their time (around 40 percent) selling in a broad sense—persuading, influencing, and convincing others to take action. Furthermore, research respondents stated that moving others to take action was critical to their professional success.[1] Author Daniel Pink calls this "non-sales selling"—convincing people to take action that doesn't require making a purchase.

Think about the top professionals you work with personally. The best teachers persuade their students (your kids) to enjoy their subjects, do their assignments, and learn the material. Good doctors are not only strong in diagnosing and recommending the right course of action, but they also are good at convincing their patients to do things that are not always inviting, such as exercising regularly or getting a colonoscopy. An effective financial planner might commit you to a long-term investing strategy when your initial desire was to buy a bigger motor home. The success of the professionals discussed above is based upon their ability to make you more successful—whether you initially like it or not!

The same is true of the service professional. Your ability to convince your customers to take action has a big impact on their success. Getting them to agree to a regular regimen of self-maintenance, convincing them it is in their best interest to follow your company's procedures regarding escalation, or committing customer executives to participate in quarterly business reviews with a look toward the future are all activities that ultimately lead to their success. Your ability to deliver on the customer promise depends upon your powers of persuasion.

Looking at it another way, when you don't help the customer make the best decisions, you are not meeting your potential.

> Flash Point: Whether you call it servicing or consulting, advising or selling, supporting or fixing, the goal is the same—to improve the success of the customer.

OK, let's shift gears and talk about the service professional's role in traditional selling—helping commit the customer to make a purchase of services, or consumables, or spare parts, hardware or software, or whatever your company offers.

I know what some of you are thinking: *Oh, jeez, Alex! You are taking this proactive stuff too far! I just like to make things run and fix them when they break...if I'd wanted to sell, I would have gone into sales.*

Let's talk about why "selling" is so distasteful for so many of us. A quick question: When you hear the word "selling," what thoughts come to mind? I've asked this question countless times in my workshops with customer-facing service providers, whatever their title. The answers are predictable: "slick," "used car salesman," and, my favorite, "sleazy."

This is truly a shame. Many of us let a few bad experiences early in our lives or stereotypes about salespeople (watch the movie *Tin Men* for a great example of all that can be bad about selling) color our thoughts and attitudes toward what is one of the most challenging and important professions.

Selling Does Not Have to Be Evil

Selling is not necessarily evil. The truth is in how we think about and define "professional selling." Figure 6.1, The Persuasion Continuum, sheds some insight about the differences between influencing with integrity (professional selling) and manipulation.

Figure 6.1

The Persuasion Continuum		
Manipulation		**Influencing with Integrity**
◄─────────────────────────────────────►		
What's in it for me?	POINT OF VIEW	What's good for the customer, my company, and me?
Personal gain	FOCUS	Creating value
Slick presentation	TECHNIQUES	Trust-building behaviors
Short-term transaction	TIME HORIZON	Long-term relationship
Biggest moneymaker	DESIRED ROLE	Trusted advisor

Individuals whose persuasion philosophy is manipulation have the "What's in it for me?" point of view. They don't care whether the sale is good for the customer, as long as they get the sale. "Greed is good" is their mantra. Professional sellers, however, start with the mindset, "What's good for the customer?" They realize that creating customer value will lead to value for them and for their organization. People who live by the standard of influencing with integrity understand the old maxim, "You've got to give to get."

The manipulator relies on a slick presentation as the chosen technique for success. Formula selling skills (Attention-Interest-Desire-Action is a classic example) are used as an attempt to trigger buying behavior (push buttons) in order to coerce the prospect into buying whatever the seller wants to sell—whether the buyer needs it or not. Sellers who influence with integrity, on the other hand, put a very high value on their personal reputation. Therefore, they prefer honest dialogue as their communication technique of choice. Providing straight talk about problems and fixes, what they know, and what they don't know, these folks tell it like it is because their personal credibility is on the line.

The time horizon of the manipulator is "right now." He or she is only interested in making today's numbers, this month's numbers, and the quarterly numbers. Nothing else counts. "Live for today" is the motto of the manipulator. Conversely, professionals who influence with integrity are in it for the long haul. Sure, they welcome quick purchases that are good for the customer, but they will not jeopardize their customer's trust for short-term gain. They (hopefully) will be coming back to the customer again and again. They know that a long-term relationship takes time and effort, but is worth the investment.

Finally, manipulators want to be showcased to their peers as the biggest moneymakers—the top dogs—at the annual sales extravaganza in Hawaii. This is the ultimate recognition and the role they lust after. However, the brilliant service professional's recognition comes from being seen as a trusted advisor. Nothing epitomizes success more than this achievement. When your customers call you over the weekend to ask your advice about an important personal issue that is totally non-related to business, you know you have reached this level of trust. It is an awesome feeling.

So the next time you hear the word "selling," don't be too quick to judge. If it is meant as the professional, influencing-with-integrity type of selling described above, respect the phrase for all it implies. In the best businesses, everybody who touches the customer sells, and they are proud of it.[2]

Flash Point: If a customer has an issue that you have the potential to effectively address, you are not acting as a professional unless you try to help her.

Everyone Sells Everything

In elite organizations, everyone who has contact with the customer (or prospect, or partner, or supplier, or the media, or anyone) understands that an important part of their job responsibility is to "sell" their organization, its capabilities, and the offerings it provides — the receptionist who makes everyone feel comfortable and welcome, the technical support specialist who doesn't treat you like an idiot and really cares about your problem, the finance person who takes the trouble to understand your needs and demonstrates a little flexibility. Organizations that embed that philosophy into their culture stand head and shoulders above their competitors.[3]

What Service Executives Expect of Their Service Professionals Regarding Selling

As you will recall, many comments from the services executives in my research referenced in Chapter 1 talked a lot about the importance of having their service professionals help sell.[4] Specifically, I asked them to define their selling expectations for their service professionals by choosing one of the six levels of selling displayed in Figure 6.2. As you will see, a service professional operating at Level 1 has no role in selling, but the expectation and involvement increases as you move to each higher level.

Here are Shining Examples for each level of a service pro-

Figure 6.2

The Six Levels of Selling Expectations for Technical Experts

1. Focus on fixing problems and meeting services objectives and leaving all sales tasks to others.
2. When the customer mentions potential opportunities, communicate these opportunities to the appropriate person.
3. Actively look and listen for customer opportunities, then pass them on to the appropriate person.
4. Actively look and listen for customer opportunities, qualify the customer need, then pass them on to the appropriate person.
5. Actively look, listen, and research opportunities, qualify the need, and work with the appropriate person to develop proposals.
6. Actively look, listen, and research customer opportunities, qualify the need, develop the proposal, and present it to the customer.

---

fessional's possible communication to a salesperson about Big Bucks Bank:

*   **Level 1:** "Hi Jim. Just a quick update to let you know that the service project is on track. Hope your golf game is improving."
*   **Level 2:** "Hi Jim. I overheard Billie Owens, the senior vice president at Big Bucks Bank, complain to one of her people about how limited their web solution process was. Thought you'd like to know."
*   **Level 3:** "Hi Jim. In my weekly debriefing with Billie Owens, the senior vice president at Big Bucks Bank, I asked her what other technical problems were giving her fits. The attached document outlines what she said her five biggest systems problems were. Go get 'em!"
*   **Level 4:** "Hi Jim. In my weekly debriefing with Billie Owens, the senior vice president at Big Bucks Bank, I asked her what other technical systems problems were giving her fits. She outlined five issues that were her biggest challenges. I then proceeded to qualify those challenges and found that

there were two issues she was serious about acting upon that I think we could handle quite well. Attached are my qualifying checklists for these two needs and a few notes. Good luck."

- **Level 5:** "Hi Jim. In my weekly debriefing with Billie Owens, the senior vice president at Big Bucks Bank, I asked her what other problems were giving her fits. She outlined five issues that were her biggest challenges. I then proceeded to qualify those challenges and found that there were two issues she was serious about acting upon. Attached are my notes. What does your schedule look like for Tuesday? Maybe we can set aside 45 minutes to plan our approach and create a proposal for these two new potential projects?"
- **Level 6:** "Hi Jim. Just wanted to keep you in the loop. I'm pleased to say that Billie Owens, the senior vice president at Big Bucks Bank, has agreed to two more projects! Attached you'll find the signed agreements and project plans. You'll note that the first one starts in two weeks. Your commission may be enough to get that new driver you've been lusting for! Let me know if you have any questions."

Take a minute and think about your own management's current expectations of your role in selling. What level are you at today? Where do you think you should be tomorrow? Now compare that to what those executives expected that are shown in Figure 6.3. As you see, the expectations were very high, with most executives wanting their service people to be very aggressive in helping get new business.

Caveats to Consider

This question in the research was about the general selling expectations of technical experts. However, there are some caveats to consider. For example, many executives were quite aggressive in their selling expectations when it came to service contracts,

Figure 6.3

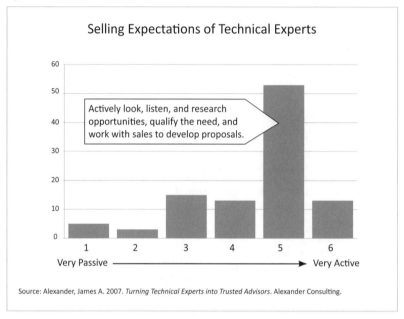

but most had lower expectations of service professionals help-ing to sell products, e.g., hardware or software. In most of these cases, they wanted the technical expert to pass it over to sales or the appropriate person. However, for those executives from or-ganizations that sold consumables or spare parts, many wanted their service pros to be at a Level 6 — to actually sell and take the order themselves. Therefore, a more refined and more practical approach for implementation in a specific services business is to define the selling expectation for each type of offering, for each category of service professional.

When I consult with service executives on this topic, I recom-mend just that — establish core expectations for various services personnel groups for each offering and build that into their job description. Once the core expectation is set, higher expectations can be established for those individuals who are willing and able to be more engaged in helping to sell. Ideally, these individuals should make more money, as they are adding more value to the customer and to the company. Of course, if you are striving to become a BSP, you should be at the highest level appropriate for your situation.

Rarely would I recommend Level 1 or Level 2, and many times Level 3 is appropriate, but Level 4 makes the most sense as a core recommendation the majority of the time.

Qualifying Great Business

The difference between Level 3 and Level 4 is that Level 4 requires that you qualify the opportunity to make certain that what the customer needs is something that your organization can deliver. Hence, to qualify an opportunity, you need to have both technical acumen related to all of your capabilities, products, and services, and you need to have the customer acumen discussed in Chapter 3.

Brilliant Practice: The Cup of Coffee Conversation

Let's assume that you have just finished a successful service engagement (installing, implementing, repairing, maintaining) and the customer is satisfied. Now is the time to proactively qualify customer opportunities using the Four I's Qualifying Strategy, shown in Figure 6.4.

In this scenario, your Shining Example conversation might go something like this:

BSP: "Mr. Customer, how about a 10-minute coffee break? If you don't mind, I'm interested in learning more about your business."

Customer: "Sure! In fact, I'll buy!"

BSP: "Thanks, Phil. Tell me, what are the main issues you and your department are facing?"

Customer: "Well, the whole company is tasked with introducing Lean manufacturing principles, so I am involved in that. I am having a difficult time finding qualified candidates for opera-

Figure 6.4

Qualifying Great Business
The Four I's Qualifying Strategy

Issues → Importance → Impact → Investigate

- What are the main **issues** you and your department are facing?
- Let's take a look at XXX for a moment. Is this a nice-to-do or is it something **important** to your organization?
- Sounds critical. Tell me, what is the **impact** of not addressing this problem?
- I see. Together, how may we **investigate** how we might be able to help?

tor positions, and I have to figure out how to boost the productivity of my three biggest lines by at least 20 percent."

BSP: "Thank you for that. Let's take a look at your productivity challenge for a moment. Is that a nice-to-do or is it something important to your organization?"

Customer: "Yes, it is very important to making my numbers for the year."

BSP: "Sounds critical. Let me ask, what is the impact if you don't reach your productivity goals?"

Customer (frowning, with blood draining from his face): "It is not a pretty sight...you see, my bonus depends upon making that productivity goal. I promised the kids a trip to Disney World, and there is no way I can afford it without my bonus. I have to make that target."

BSP: "I see. Together, may we investigate how our organization might be able to help?"

Customer: "Sure!"

So if you're thinking that this sounds great, but you just don't have time to invest in this type of interrogatory, consider this: In the time it takes to drink a cup of coffee, you can qualify an opportunity that is important to the customer and fits your company's capabilities. If none of the issues that the customer views as priorities are a good fit for your company, then just enjoy the conversation while you build your customer acumen.

Most of the time, whether a good opportunity arises or not, the customer appreciates the conversation because (a) he is doing most of the talking, (b) he is talking about something important to him, and (c) you are demonstrating that you care and that you want to help.

Sounds like a no-lose situation to me.

The Decision Triangle

In Chapter 3, Customer Acumen, we talked about the importance of both understanding business issues to determine the best technical solutions and communicating in the business speak appropriate for different individuals performing different functions and roles within the customer company. Now it is time

Figure 6.5

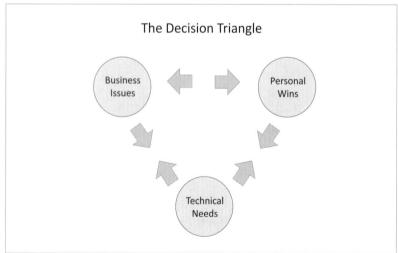

to add the third leg to this three-sided triangle: Personal Wins.

The Decision Triangle, seen in Figure 6.5, shows that business issues, technical needs, and personal wins are all connected. Finding the technical needs that best address the business issues is critical, but it is not enough; personal wins must be factored into the persuasion formula.

It is up to the BSP to understand that connection in order to shape conversations that can best help the customer. Personal wins take into consideration, "What's in it for me?" from the customer's personal standpoint.

Figure 6.6

Just as business issues vary by company and department, personal wins vary by the individual. A straightforward way to categorize personal wins is seen in Figure 6.6, and can be described as follows:

- **Achievement.** Individuals who put a high value on achievement strive to meet or exceed personal objectives. The personal pride of doing something well is a big motivator for them.
- **Recognition.** Individuals who crave recognition are always looking for ways to look good in front of the boss and others. They are interested in any opportunity to enhance their positive notoriety.

- **Power.** People who are motivated by power are constantly on the lookout for ways to increase their influence or expand their control. As a sterling example of power lusting, take a look at your elected officials.
- **Enjoyment.** People with high enjoyment needs like to have fun. They might enjoy dealing with likeable peers they respect, working with a highly esteemed customer, or just doing something different.

When customers understand that what you are recommending gives them more of what they crave, the probability of their acceptance goes up.

Brilliant Practice: Show them how acting on your advice will give them the personal win they desire.

Here are some Shining Examples that address the various personal wins important to customers:

- For a customer with a high need for achievement: "Wow! When this project is up and running, it will blow the doors off your KPIs!"
- For a customer with a high need for recognition: "I had another customer who led an innovative project similar to what we are talking about. Along with contributing impressive results, he was given a special award from his company's chairman. Would you like to see the write-up he received in his company's magazine?"
- For a customer with a high need for power: "If this project goes as well as we both believe, it will probably drive the creation of a whole new business unit—someone will have to lead it. Maybe you?"
- For a customer with a high need for enjoyment: "Harry, I'm excited. I really like working with cool new technologies, really smart folks, and doing things seldom done before. How about you?"

However, some other factors can mediate the attractiveness of the personal wins, including safety, structure, and simplicity.

Safety

Some people will go to great lengths to avoid personal risk. They much prefer the tried and true, the status quo. They are the "you never get fired for hiring IBM" kind of folks.

Brilliant Practice: If your customer has high safety needs, point out the low-risk attributes of your recommendation.

A Shining Example would be: "Mr. Customer, I admit that we have never implemented this solution in your industry. However, we have four years of proven experience in implementing this solution in other industries facing similar challenges. I have a plan to ensure that our project will deliver as anticipated. May I walk you through my suggestions?"

Structure

Some customers like to follow established rules. They are open to new ideas, but only if they fit in or complement the existing framework of "how things are done around here."

Brilliant Practice: If your customer has high structure needs, point out how what you recommend complements what she is already doing.

A Shining Example to address this type of person might sound like this: "Hello, Sue. The nice part about our Brilliant Services training is that the principles taught in the course complement and reinforce the skills that are in The Seven Habits training that everyone has been through. I'm sure that your executives will appreciate the synergy this will bring."

Simplicity

There is one other mediating factor important to anyone considering a buying decision, and that is simplicity. I am a firm believer that buying should be easy — I bet you share that belief as well. For example, when I am shopping online for just about anything, the first place I look is Amazon. Why? Because they make it so easy. If I am in a hurry, two clicks and I am done. If I want to look at reviews posted by other consumers of the product I am considering, just one more click takes me there. If I want to see what else others like me have purchased, one more click is all it takes. This is a prime reason why Amazon has become a dominant Internet player. Most businesses could noticeably improve quickly by embracing the concept of simplicity.

Brilliant Practice: Minimize hassle. Make the buying process as easy as possible.

Here's a Shining Example: "Tom, I appreciate you championing the project. We both agree that it can make a big impact and make us all look good! However, I know that there is a lot of effort required to make a change of this type within your company, and I am committed to making things simple and easy. May we talk through what must be done and together work out ways to make things as painless as possible?"

Ideally, business issues and personal wins are related. For example, implementing innovative software effectively in the hope of creating competitive advantage will match up well with a person who finds personal enjoyment in creativity and is not shy when it comes to risk. Changing a process to improve uptime aligns well with a person's desire for achievement, and so on.

Flash Point: Personal wins trump business issues every time.

Unless there are large differences in the potential business impact of different choices, people make decisions first based upon personal wins; then they work to demonstrate the required business issue impact (using return on investment, total cost of ownership, net present value, or whatever) to justify their decision.

Here's a personal example: Many years ago as a young professional, I was in the market for a new car to use for business purposes. For me, a personal win was a 5-Series BMW. I wanted the recognition of success associated with that strong brand and the fun I was sure I would have driving it. Even before walking into the showroom, I could envision the oohs and ahhs of other drivers as I zipped by. Was a Bimmer the most practical and efficient option? Could I have purchased a much less-expensive car that would have gotten me here and there safely and comfortably? Of course. But I wanted that midnight-blue 528e with the moon roof and awesome tune machine.

However, once my emotional mind was made up, the rational mind kicked in. I had to justify the car to my wife (and to me) from a practical, logical standpoint. I told her why my choice addressed some of the "business issues" related to my decision, such as:

- It is rated high in safety so we could be assured of maximum protection in the event of an accident.
- BMWs have a history of excellent resale value, so this was a solid investment.
- It gets good gas mileage for a car in its category.
- The doors open wide so that your mother can easily get in and out.
- We will park way at the back of parking lots to lessen the possibility of dings, so we will walk more and be healthier.
- Making that big payment each month will motivate me to make more money and thus take better care of my family.

Well, you get the picture. As I explained all of these practical benefits, my wife nodded her head sagely, knowing full well that this was all baloney. She wanted the car too! She and I colluded to justify this not-so-practical purchase. Now tell me you have never done that! And buyers making business decisions do the same thing.

Stakeholder Analysis

If you are in the persuasion business (you are), then understanding and relating the value of your offerings to the business issues and personal needs of your customers is critical. Also, note that the more expensive/important/risky the purchase, the greater the number of people that will be involved in the decision. For example, in the technology industry, on average, 12 people from the customer are actively involved in making solution-buying decisions.[5]

Figure 6.7

Stakeholder Analysis EXAMPLE

STAKEHOLDER	TITLE	ROLE	BUSINESS ISSUES	PERSONAL WINS
Philip Thomas	CIO	Decision Maker	Maximize uptime. Demonstrate financial impact.	Peer recognition as innovator. Minimal hassle.
Suzanne Bio	IT Manager	Influencer	System failures. Minimize downtime.	Waiting for retirement. Don't rock the boat.
Bubba Gomez	Network Admin.	Influencer	Minimize downtime. Loves cool technology.	Wants to be promoted. Likes to be in control.

The Stakeholder Analysis is a simple, powerful, and necessary tool to help you better understand your customers, so you can better help your customers. Figure 6.7 shows an example of three key stakeholders (in reality, there were five more) from an existing customer company exploring ways to improve their network performance. You see that Philip Thomas is the CIO, and in this case was the decision maker in selecting a supplier to purchase a network solution from. Typically, the decision maker is the person with the budget and the implementation ownership of the purchase. From a business standpoint, Philip is interested in maximizing the uptime of the network and being able to show the financial impact of implementing the solution. Personally, Philip wants his peers—other CIOs—to recognize him as an innovator. Furthermore, he loathes hassle. Thus, when you communicate with Philip about your recommendations, you would be wise to stress how it will reduce downtime and show strong financial improvement. Also, indicate the recognition opportunities and emphasize how simple and easy it will be to implement.

Figure 6.7 also shows the key factors important to the IT manager, an important influencer in the decision, and also those of a user, the network administrator. Even though the decision maker has the budget and is responsible for results, most com-

Figure 6.8

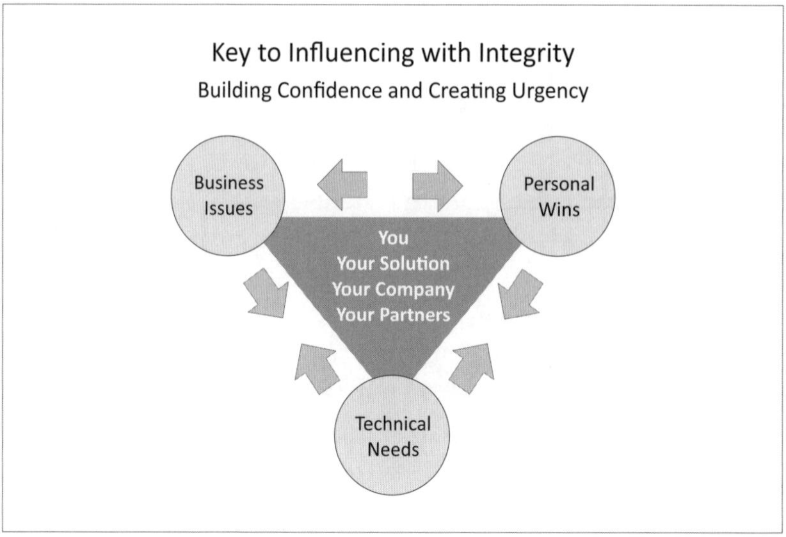

Key to Influencing with Integrity
Building Confidence and Creating Urgency

Business Issues

Personal Wins

You
Your Solution
Your Company
Your Partners

Technical Needs

panies have someone who acts as the "approver," reviewing and then blessing the decision maker's planned purchase.

So whenever you are helping your company acquire more business, by yourself or as part of a team, I suggest that you use this tool (or something similar) to help you better understand how you build customer confidence and urgency by showing how your recommendations positively impact the customer's technical needs to meet both their business issues and the personal wins of key players (Figure 6.8). The end result: The customer will see enough value, emotionally and rationally, in what you are recommending to outweigh the costs associated with getting benefits.

The Value Teeter-Totter

When it comes to selling, the elixir of life, the Rosetta stone of understanding, the guiding light of focus is the ability to create and demonstrate value. More than almost any other capability, this skill is a core driver of success for your customers and profitable growth for your company.

So, let's begin at the beginning with the question, "Just what is value?" What you have learned so far in this book is that value is what the customer says it is. It is unique for every customer, because the business issues and personal needs vary from company to company and from person to person.

Figure 6.9, The Value Teeter-Totter, shows a simple way to envision a value-creating model. Here is how it works:

1. Based upon what you know about the customer's business issues and personal wins, list the most important benefits (addressing their business issues and personal wins) that they hope to achieve on the left-hand side of the teeter-totter.
2. Benefits are rarely free. On the right-hand side are the three components of cost that every potential customer considers: the actual money to be spent, the time that will elapse before gaining the benefits, and the amount of hassle required to

Figure 6.9

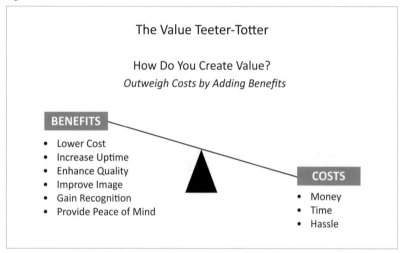

The Value Teeter-Totter

How Do You Create Value?
Outweigh Costs by Adding Benefits

BENEFITS
- Lower Cost
- Increase Uptime
- Enhance Quality
- Improve Image
- Gain Recognition
- Provide Peace of Mind

COSTS
- Money
- Time
- Hassle

make the purchase and implement the recommendation.

3. So just like a teeter-totter in a playground, your task is to show the customer that the potential benefits greatly outweigh the anticipated costs. You use your customer acumen, trust builders, and relationship skills to tip the balance in the customer's mind.

Flash Point: Although rarely spoken, anticipated personal hassle is the biggest deterrent to buying.

Yes, money is important, but all sorts of studies show that financial cost is way down on the list of factors of why people don't buy. When you hear, "Your price is just too high," realize that in most cases, the prospect is lying. It is much easier and more convenient (and less painful) to fabricate this "too expensive" excuse than to confess that you just don't want to take the time or put up with the hassle (e.g., making numerous presentations trying to get naysayers on the board to agree to the purchase or putting in the hours needed internally to justify the change). Although rarely spoken, anticipated personal hassle is the biggest deterrent to buying. In the short term, it's always easier to maintain the status quo than to rock the boat, no matter how logical the answers or how dramatic the potential impact.

Brilliant Practice: Take away the pain, keep things simple, and good decisions are much more likely to be made.

Act like a heavyweight and tip the teeter-totter so that benefits greatly outweigh the cost, and the customer will do the right thing—that is what influencing with integrity is all about.

Now it's time to put it all together, taking all that you have learned to proactively lead brilliant customer conversations introduced in the next chapter.

CHAPTER 7

Putting It All Together

Leading Brilliant Conversations

In this chapter, we put it all together using the seven trust builders, our customer acumen, and the four core relationship skills, enabling you to lead brilliant conversations with customers, your internal colleagues, and executives of all stripes.

You will be introduced to the 80-20 rule and a Brilliant Conversation Checklist that will frame your preparation. You will learn how to guide and control a conversation without appearing to, how to tangiblize the intangible, and how to make it easy for the customer to commit to action. You will see how the proper influencing tools can make your job much, much easier. Brilliant Practices and Shining Examples will provide a framework for applying this road map back at your job.

You will discover that the same communication approaches used with customers can (and should) be applied inside your organization to convince people to do the right things, including selling sales on selling services. Finally, you will learn about the special requirements of conversing with and influencing executives.

The content of this chapter should only be applied when the customer's emotions are on the left side of the Emotion Meter, seen in Figure 7.1, and he is open to talking about the future.

Figure 7.1

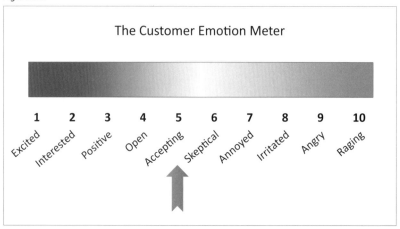

The 80-20 Rule

When people are interested in the topic of a conversation, they prefer to talk much more than they prefer to listen. They will give their opinions, share their thinking, and give numerous personal examples, often going on and on with excitement. In fact, if they have a willing communication partner, they will dominate the conversation, talking roughly 80 percent of the time. Yikes! This violates the law of fairness! Be that as it may, this is reality.

So, what does that mean to the brilliant service professional? It means that if we want to show respect and be seen as an excellent conversationalist, then we need to make sure we allow the customer to talk as much as they'd like. Therefore, if the customer wants to talk 80 percent of the time, then we will have to listen 80 percent of the time — listening with intensity, focused on every word, positively reacting to every statement. The vital side benefit is that along with deepening the relationship, properly focused listening will help you gain a deep understanding of the customer's business issues and personal wins — must-have components before making recommendations persuasive enough to move the customer off the status quo.

The only way to conform to the 80-20 rule is to ask primarily "open probes," encouraging the customer to talk all they want. The Brilliant Conversation Checklist will help ensure that this occurs.

The Brilliant Conversation Checklist

Your job is to steer, guide, and nudge the customer toward taking positive action that improves her business and personal situation. As I have emphasized throughout the book, preparation is vital before any customer interaction. For proactive conversations, Figure 7.2 shows the 10 planning steps I recommend. We start by tapping into our personal experience and the information contained in your knowledge management system.

Figure 7.2

The Brilliant Conversation Checklist

1. Understand the customer's business issues.
2. Anticipate the customer's personal wins.
3. Set conversation objectives.
4. Develop the positioning statement.
5. Establish planned probes.
6. Consider relevant what-why-benefits.
7. Anticipate concerns and appropriate responses.
8. Prepare influencing tools.
9. Visualize success.
10. Relax.

Step 1: Understand the Customer's Business Issues

As we discussed in Chapter 3, it all starts with customer acumen—knowing the customer's business, how they work, how they think, what their strategy is, and what their problems and opportunities are. Clearly defining the customer's business issues provides you with a rational target upon which to best illustrate the value your products and services can bring.

Step 2: Anticipate the Customer's Personal Wins

At the same time we consider the customer's business issues, we need to understand and consider the personal wins of the key stakeholders to be involved in the upcoming conversation. This is our emotional target that we must address.

The primary tool for helping you complete Steps 1 and 2 is the Stakeholder Analysis, introduced in Chapter 6.

Flash Point: If you don't know, don't go! Find out the customer's business issues and/or personal wins before holding the conversation.

Step 3: Set Conversation Objectives

When we act like a BSP, every conversation should: (1) make you smarter by learning more about your customer, and (2) deepen the customer relationship as a result of practicing the seven trust builders and the four core relationship skills.

Obviously, both of these are valuable outcomes, but our main conversation focus is to influence with integrity to move the customer toward greater success. Good objectives require that the customer take action, investing her time and/or her money.

Primary Objective

Your primary objective is to get the biggest commitment possible that day. Like any good objective, it should be specific, realistic, and measurable. For example, if you are an FSE planning a customer conversation, your primary objective might be to commit your customer to a Platinum service contract. Or, depending upon your company's role definitions, your appropriate objective might be to get the customer to commit to speak with your salesperson about service contracts.

A good objective for a support engineer might well be to get a "problem child" customer to agree to follow your company's escalation process. A service account manager might want to gain customer commitment to add a resident engineer from your company to work full time at a key customer facility. A technical consultant might try to move the customer to agree to a technology assessment. All of the above are specific and measurable. If you know the customer well, then your recommendations are realistic. You have to decide what is most relevant, but set your sights on the highest value-contributing action first.

Back-Up Objective

Sometimes achieving you primary objective is not possible; therefore, you should have a back-up objective. A back-up objective still requires the customer to take action, but it is not as big a commitment and possibly is seen as less risky to the customer. For example, your primary objective might be to get the customer to put all of your products under a service contract, but your back-up objective might be a pilot or proof of concept—putting the products at one location under contract. Because of the smaller investment and limited scope, the customer might well see this option as lower risk, and thus be more willing to commit.

In another situation, your primary objective might be to convince the customer to upgrade their software. Your back-up objective might be to commit them to a two-hour demo, which will enable them to see the potential value more clearly. This is still a commitment of time, but no financial investment is required.

Another potential back-up objective might be committing the customer to an audit, comparing the existing performance of their process against world-class standards. This could quantify probable value, such as ROI, and demonstrate that your customer is practicing appropriate due diligence and managing risk.

Step 4: Develop a Positioning Statement

A positioning statement helps you take control of the conversation without appearing to. After a few moments of trust-building chit-chat, it is time to focus the conversation. Positioning starts the conversation right by targeting a topic that you want to discuss and that you feel the customer sees as important.

Three effective ways to position a conversation are by presenting, probing, or predicting. Presenting provides a strong rationale for the discussion, probing immediately invites the customer to contribute to the exploration of the issue, and predicting shows your credibility about a customer problem or an opportunity. All three can be very effective.

Because of its importance, I strongly recommend that you write out your positioning statement and practice it before heading into the conversation.

Here's a Shining Example to use when positioning your conversation by presenting the what-why-benefit: "What I'd like to do is talk about some of your priorities for the next six months. Why I suggest this is to be proactive in our preparation and minimize any unwelcome surprises. The benefit to you will be a much higher probability of achieving your goals. Sound OK?"

This is an appropriate Shining Example when positioning your conversation through probing: "Mr. Customer, when we talked on the phone, you said you where pondering making some changes with your CRM. What is your thinking?"

When it comes to positioning your conversation by means of predicting, this Shining Example is a good one: "Mr. Customer, in working with a number of senior managers like you, I am seeing some patterns emerge. I'd predict that demonstrating the business value of your IT investments is one of your top three priorities. It that correct?"

Step 5: Establish Planned Probes

While you have your pen in hand or your fingers on your keyboard, write out a few open probes that can be used in almost any situation during the conversation so that if you have a "Florida Moment" (your mind goes blank for no apparent reason), you can peek down at your notes and ask a probe that keeps the conversation going and allows you time to get back on track. Writing your questions down ahead of time allows you to focus on listening and not worrying about what you will say. Having a few open probes such as "Oh?", "Please say more," and "What was your thinking?" a glance away are great stress reducers.

Step 6: Consider Relevant What-Why-Benefits

In Step 3, when formulating your objectives, you had to consider what recommendations might be most appropriate. Now is the time to think through the why and the probable benefits of that recommendation to the customer.

Ideally, your company should have standard what-why-benefit profiles (sometimes called feature-benefit-result profiles) for all your major offerings. Figure 7.3 shows an example what-why-benefit profile for an assessment service. It shows the characteristics and resulting value of the most important aspects of the offering.

If your company does not provide these profiles, I suggest you take the initiative and create your own, using your experience and that of others to list all possible what-why-benefits for each important service and product. From there, consider your customer's business issues and personal wins to select those most relevant and tailor them to your customer.

We covered this concept earlier in the book, but it deserves

Figure 7.3

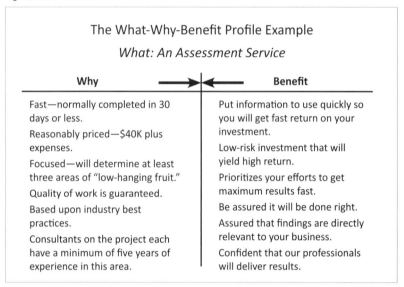

The What-Why-Benefit Profile Example

What: An Assessment Service

Why	Benefit
Fast—normally completed in 30 days or less.	Put information to use quickly so you will get fast return on your investment.
Reasonably priced—$40K plus expenses.	Low-risk investment that will yield high return.
Focused—will determine at least three areas of "low-hanging fruit."	Prioritizes your efforts to get maximum results fast.
Quality of work is guaranteed.	Be assured it will be done right.
Based upon industry best practices.	Assured that findings are directly relevant to your business.
Consultants on the project each have a minimum of five years of experience in this area.	Confident that our professionals will deliver results.

a reminder: True professionals resist the temptation to jump on the soapbox and expound and expand once they have the slightest sniff of a customer issue. The BSP only gives advice after: (1) having a thorough understanding of the customer's current situation, past history, business challenges and opportunities, and the personal implications of action and non-action, and (2) the customer knows that you know. At this point, your probing with purpose and listening with intensity has paid off, and you have earned the right to present.

Step 7: Anticipate Concerns and Appropriate Responses

When being proactive, welcome resistance…it is a sign that the customer is interested. It is common and natural that the customer will show some resistance to change when considering the recommendations you present. Even though what you recommend is rational and right, the customer's initial response will be to defend and delay — defend the way things are today and delay change tomorrow; hence the importance of being prepared, handling the concerns calmly and confidently, and not taking things personally.

The good news is that there are only a few basic concerns that will arise the majority of the time. Figure 7.4 highlights the broad category of concerns to expect and gives a Shining Example as to

Figure 7.4

Acknowledging Concerns

Brilliant Conversation Examples

Customer: "Your prices are quite a bit higher than your competitors' prices."
Brilliant Service Professional:
1. Remain calm.
2. Pause before responding.
3. Express your understanding: "I understand, price is important. Our organization is committed to delivering the highest return on your investment."
4. Indicate what you plan to do about it: "Let's take a look at all the costs in detail to see what is best for you."

Customer: "We are going to put Phase 2 out to bid."
Brilliant Service Professional:
1. Remain calm.
2. Pause before responding.
3. Express your understanding: "Sure, I know what corporate policy is."
4. Indicate what you plan to do about it: "Let me suggest that you use the specifications that we've already developed. We know they are an excellent fit, and it will save you time and hassle."

Customer: "That sounds too good to be true!"
Brilliant Service Professional:
1. Remain calm.
2. Pause before responding.
3. Express your understanding: "It does, doesn't it?"
4. Indicate what you plan to do about it: "Let me show you an example of an organization with a situation similar to yours..."

Customer: "Your competitors say you have a good product, but are not capable of solutions. I didn't know you offered solutions, too."
Brilliant Service Professional:
1. Remain calm.
2. Pause before responding.
3. Express your understanding: "That's interesting. We've been working in this area successfully for seven years. "
4. Indicate what you plan to do about it: "May I share with you what we've learned?"

how to deal with each one. Follow the model when dealing with other concerns you face. Practice responding using the words you feel comfortable with.

You will note that each of the concerns mentioned requires "proof" to back up what you have stated. Several influencing tools in the next section will work well as proof sources when needed.

Step 8: Prepare Influencing Tools

In the hands of a capable photographer, a quality camera equipped with a charged battery, a fast memory card, and a 50mm lens will be all that is needed to deliver quality photos in many situations. However, the thoughtful photographer will be prepared for situations that are more challenging, complementing his camera with a quality tripod, backup memory cards and batteries, lighting equipment, and a host of lenses.

A thoughtful conversationalist takes the same approach. He arms himself with tools that will help him deal with various situations that might come up in a discussion.

I am using the term "tool" to include virtually anything that aids the BSP in persuading the customer to take action. Effective tools do one or more of the following:

- Improve understanding.
- Simplify complexity.
- Tangibilize the intangible.
- Involve the customer.
- Add credibility.
- Overcome resistance.

Anything that addresses the above list is a persuasion tool. Below I have listed the ones I feel are most valuable to the BSP.

Persuasion Tool: Analogies and Stories

Communicating stories and analogies that the customer can understand and relate to are powerful tools in getting the customer to grasp your meanings and tangibilize the intangible. In fact, I have consciously tried to use them throughout the book.

As discussed in Chapter 6, the "hassle" factor plays a big role in stopping or slowing the customer from making a change.

This Shining Example could be used to help the customer more easily relate to the point the BSP is trying to make: "I don't know about you, but I hate hassle. For example, I have not up-dated my personal insurance policies in years, even though I know I should. I just don't like the hassle and time it takes to do it. I know that your championing this project I'm recommending will add more responsibilities for you until things are up and running. I'm committed to making it as simple and easy for you as possible. I've mapped out what I think needs to be done. May I walk you through this to get your thoughts?"

Your customer may never have purchased a business assess-ment before, but he can probably relate to the need for a physical checkup before taking on a new sport or strenuous activity.

Here's a Shining Example of how to employ this analogy: "Mr. Customer, as we have talked about before, I know you enjoy go-ing to NASCAR events. Let's say you were contemplating racing cars yourself. The first step before investing big money into the necessary equipment is to have a physical examination to confirm your capability and identify any issues that might put you at risk. This step is so important that racing associations require it.

"Just like the physical exam, the assessment I recommend will confirm that it is appropriate to move ahead with the project as well as identify any potential risks that must be addressed. Doing this due diligence makes good business sense."

Furthermore, if you find yourself in a competitive position, you might take the medical analogy one step further: "In many situations, a general practitioner is adequate to perform a physi-cal examination. We are not a general practitioner; we are more similar to a heart specialist. We have deep expertise focused entirely on network performance—the type of experience needed to deal with the complexity you face."

Another analogy that customers can easily relate to involves comparing their organization's network to that of the plumbing network within a home.

Here's a Shining Example that illustrates it: "I find it useful to think about the networks we build and maintain as the plumbing in your home. The problem you face is that there are several slow leaks in your network, slowing down the flow of communication. Just like a good plumber, the first task is to identify where the leaks are."

This next Shining Example looks at how to draw an analogy from one type of service contract to another. Although your customer may never have purchased a service contract for your type of equipment, she may have purchased a service contract for her company's copiers. By asking her the reasons for her decision, she can better relate to the benefits of your service contract—benefits such as uptime, convenience, or no hassles.

BSP: "Ms. Customer, please share with me the reasons why you purchase service contracts on your copiers."

Customer: "Well, I don't want my people bothering with the equipment. Their time is better spent elsewhere."

BSP: "You will get the same benefits with our service contract, as well. For example, we take full ownership of maintaining our products, eliminating hassles for you and allowing your people to focus on more important tasks."

If the customer has no business experience with services contracts, she probably has some personal experience, such as purchasing an extended warranty on a 3D TV or other large purchase. Explore her thinking and relate it back to your offering. It may help to provide a personal example of your own as an illustration: "I purchased a new sophisticated camera and decided to get the three-year, extended, full-coverage warranty. I am really glad I did. Sixteen months after purchasing it, I dropped the camera while riding my bike. The company replaced my camera with a newer model with no questions asked, no hassle, and no cost. It turned out to be a great investment. What benefits would you like to receive from a service contract from us?"

Other non-business analogies can help bridge the non-familiarity gap as well. Sporting examples often are good choices. For example, if you know your customer is a big football fan (U.S. football), you can use football terms and concepts to relate the importance of ideas in a way the customer can easily understand.

A Shining Example would go something like this: "When things are going well and the business is stable, it makes sense to focus on continuous improvement — running the football, mixed with a few short passes. However, when the competition is in the lead and the clock is ticking down, it is time to open up and go deep. From what you have described, your game plan has to change to become more flexible if you want to win the Super Bowl in your market. If so, maybe it is time to seriously consider selling services as a game changer. What do you think?"

Analogies and stories are powerful people persuaders, but they are especially important when communicating the invisible, such as services.

Persuasion Tool: Happy Customer Proof
It is always better to have someone else toot your horn. The best tooters are respected people in companies that are highly recognized and respected by your customer.

The more complex and unfamiliar the situation is to the customer, the more she will look to peers to help her decide. If two or three well-respected people in well-respected companies with similar issues are happy with your offerings, your customer will likely be willing to accept the premise that she will be happy as well. Happy customer proof acts as a shortcut to decision making, sometimes dramatically compressing your customer's buying cycle.

Flash Point: What respected outsiders say will always carry more weight than what you say, even when you have achieved BSP status.

There are five influencing tools that use the clout of existing customers:

1. **Customer List.** Just presenting a list of name-brand customers can add credibility and imply deep experience: "We are very proud of the company we keep. Here is our financial industry customer list. You will notice some very well-known companies are our customers."

2. **Customer Performance Scores.** If you have strong customer performance scores, you can use them to impress your customers. Very high customer satisfaction or Net Promoter Scores help quantify what your customers might expect from working with you. In addition, positive customer comments add qualitative richness to your information: "Please don't take our word for it. May I share with you our latest Net Promoter Scores? There are some very specific comments about our reliability being a key factor for why they are so loyal to us."

3. **Testimonials.** Testimonials are statements from credible individuals in high-recognition accounts that tout the value of you and your offerings. Testimonials can be included in your promotional brochures or be made available on video: "Sure, I understand that this is a big move for you. Would you like to hear what other executives like you say about our organization? Let me pull up a 90-second video clip on my iPad of three customers talking about us."

4. **Case Studies.** Case studies take testimonials one step further, adding more detail to which your customers can relate. They often start with the customer situation, their opportu-

nity to improve, why they decided upon your company's recommendation, the actions that occurred, and the business results. Again, the more your customer can relate to the case, the greater the credibility and the deeper their comfort level. Hard facts and figures can help your customer build and sell his internal business case for buying from you: "I agree. Quantifiable results are a necessity to justify important investments. May I share with you a case study that demonstrates just that?"

5. **Reference Accounts.** People who like, admire, or respect you enough to take their valuable time to help you are worth their weight in diamonds. They will toot and tout — take calls from strangers, meet your prospects for lunch, and host your potential customers at their facilities. Use them sparingly, thank them lavishly, and always follow up to let them know how helpful they were in helping you get more business: "I understand and agree with putting you in contact with customers that faced similar situations. Like you, these are very busy people, and I value their time. After we have agreed to move forward, as a last step, I will give you contact information for two of our current clients who will answer any questions and confirm that we are the best choice for you."

Persuasion Tool: Financial Calculators
Financial worksheets used to determine return on investment, total cost of ownership, or other financial measures help make your concepts, capabilities, and results real. Ideally, you should have actual customer data to plug into the equation gathered from an assessment. Next best is benchmark data from other organizations in similar situations. However, a powerful approach is just to ask the customer what they think sounds realistic:

BSP: "Mr. Customer, I've shared the improvements in uptime that other customers of ours in similar situations as you have gained when under our ultimate service contract — on average,

28 percent. Based on what you know, what percentage sounds realistic for your business?"

Customer: "I'd be very happy with a 15 percent improvement."

BSP: "Sure, let's use 15 percent. You said earlier that downtime costs you $3,500 per hour, correct? OK, let's do the math...."

Persuasion Tool: Research Reports

Any study from a third-party credible source makes a good persuasion tool: "As you are well aware, Gartner is the leader in comparing the technologies of different companies. As this diagram shows, we have been recognized by them as being a stellar performer by being placed in the Magic Quadrant."

Furthermore, studies that your company conducts or sponsors may help you make your case, plus position your company as an industry thought leader. For example, many customers find it reassuring that you have enough experience supported by data to know what the best practices and benchmarks are for their industry. By asking the customer how these best practices can apply to them, it helps them to both relate cognitively and connect at an emotional level. This is a real confidence builder and something that can be made quite visible in the mind of the prospect.

Persuasion Tool: Talking Papers

If your customer conversations go well, at some point you or a team member will present a proposal, letter of engagement, or statement of work to legally commit the customer to purchase.

When dealing with important, complex, or big-ticket offerings, I suggest that you don't wait until the end to put something in writing. Neither you nor the customer like surprises, so once you have a decent understanding of the issues, impact, and importance facing the customer and have a probable solution in mind, develop and introduce a talking paper. Just like a proposal, letter of engagement, or statement of work, it should clearly state the customer's situation and demonstrate the value of action and the cost of inaction. It should outline assumptions and the suggested steps and time frames for key activities, plus recommend what the customer and your organization do and don't do.

Ideally, it should use the customer's own words whenever possible and include illustrative figures and diagrams as well as a story or an analogy, if appropriate. It might also contain positive quotes from existing customers, and clearly state your guarantee (if you have one). The main difference between a talking paper and the other documents listed above is that the talking paper does not include pricing—the cost-benefit discussion is for later on. The focus of the talking paper is to confirm areas of agreement and uncover any differences of understanding before legalizing the arrangement. It can also stimulate collaboration on how you and your main sponsor can commit other key players internally.

Persuasion Tool: Whiteboarding

A powerful tool to stimulate thought and build collaboration is whiteboarding, whereby you and your customer sketch out processes, models, or diagrams on a whiteboard (or blackboard, flip chart, napkin, et al) to visually think through current situations and possible future changes.

For example, you might illustrate an ideal process, and then ask your customer to comment on where his current process is today. You might say, "Mr. Customer, may I draw out what we have found is often the ideal process for this type of manufacturing?" Then go to the whiteboard and quickly sketch it out. Next, hand the customer the marker and add, "Mind showing me where you are today?"

From there, the customer might agree on an ideal customer process for his business, and then identify the disconnects to achieving it. Inviting the customer to share his thinking goes a long way toward building confidence in you and your commitment to the collaboration.

In complex situations that the customer has not faced before, it can be very helpful to share a proposed methodology flow chart to explain your intent and let the customer think through how it might work in her organization. Properly done, it can also simplify complexity and clarify ambiguity by describing each action and the rationale of each step. Once the customer understands, you can collaborate with him to tailor your approach to his specific issues and needs: "Here is our established methodology that has proven very successful. Every situation is unique, however. May we walk through it to discover what needs to be tweaked?"

Persuasion Tool: Social Media
Even customers you have worked with for years may turn to social media to learn how others view you. It is your responsibility to represent yourself in the most appropriate manner. Take time to create a solid profile, get a professional photo, connect with colleagues, and contribute to groups. It makes a difference.

Persuasion Tool: Seven Trust Builders
Finally, let's not forget the most powerful influencing tools you have: the seven trust builders. Review them before every meeting and think about how you might use them in the conversation.

Influencing tools are important—they can turn skepticism into confidence and no into yes. Be prepared to use them in every conversation.

Step 9: Visualize Success
Just like a champion athlete, the BSP takes a couple of minutes right before a conversation to visualize success in her mind. She might picture the customer standing up with a grin as wide as

the Grand Canyon, grasping your hand saying, "Let's do it!" She might envision the customer saying, "This is just what we need! Let me see if the Big Boss is available right now," as he beams and reaches for the phone.

Step 10: Relax
Visualizing a successful outcome will naturally relax you, but in addition, it may unconsciously clear your mind and slow your thinking. Thirty seconds of deep breathing does wonders.

The Brilliant Conversation Checklist should be followed before every important conversation. A lot of effort, you say? My response is: If the conversation is important, it deserves your best effort. If the conversation is not important, don't complete the checklist…in fact, if the conversation is not important, don't have it.

Leading Brilliant Internal Conversations: Getting the People within Your Company to Do the Right Thing

Rightly so, the emphasis of this chapter and of this book is customer-focused. However, if you have been in your profession for any length of time, you know that to consistently do the right thing for the customer, you must have the ongoing support of the rest of the organization—a boss who will back you up when you do the right (although controversial) thing, technical experts on your team who reprioritize their efforts to address the critical issues of your customers, and executives who walk the services talk.

The key to getting this support is the same as when working with customers—proactively establishing relationships and building trust. Don't assume that internal people will automatically understand the value you bring; you must proactively work on getting that message across.

So whether it is engineering, the support desk, another service group, finance, marketing, or your boss, use the Brilliant Conversation Checklist when you need to persuade internally to do what's right for the customer. Show the other person what's in it for them, and why what you are recommending positively addresses the business issues and personal wins we all crave.

For example, for many support professionals, the sales organization is a key to success. When sales sells the wrong thing or sets the wrong customer expectations, services suffer (often for years). This negative impact is deepened when sales views themselves as princes and looks upon service personnel as servants there to do their bidding—just get the product up and working, fix it fast when it breaks, and then stay out of the way.

Instead of just complaining about the sales team over beverages at your yearly service meeting, be proactive and do something about it. Look for ways to help sellers do what they most want—to sell more products, and to sell them easier and faster. It seems obvious that if the customer is happy with your service, then they'll be much more likely to stay a customer and buy more. But to many sellers, it is not as clear. Set up personal meetings, ask to be at sales meetings, drop them notes regarding opportunities to sell…whatever it takes to get them on your team. Use your trust-building behaviors and your relationship skills to demonstrate your value and get sellers serious about selling services.

You may never be seen by sales as a fellow prince, but properly done, you can be seen as a wizard, advising them on how to become more successful.

Leading the Brilliant Executive Conversation

Executives are those busy, no-nonsense folks responsible for the health of their organizations. These top managers are focused on addressing the few, critical business issues of their companies that, if handled correctly, make a significant organizational impact.

As discussed in the Introduction, services leaders want to get their BSPs in front of executives—both within customers and within their own company. And for good reason: Just like customers, executives trust service guys more than anyone else, and thus the service professional's advice can have a big impact. However, conversing with executives requires a different approach.

Techniques found successful in dealing at lower levels of the organization just don't cut it when on the helm. For example, starting an initial meeting with a department head with the statement, "Tell me about your critical issues," may yield good results and start positioning you as a service professional. However, the busy exec who has no time or desire to educate the uneducated will grimace when confronted with this probe. He expects you to know his issues and their importance before having a conversation. He expects anyone seeking an audience to assume the role of consultant from the first minute of the first meeting, bringing fresh and useful information relevant to the goals and strategy of the overall organization. Only then will he consider taking his valuable time to share with you his issues and ideas. It's not that executives don't necessarily care; it is that they don't have time for the nitty-gritty. Their job is to plot the course and navigate the ship—not buy the supplies or maintain the vessel.

Brilliant Practices: Connecting with Executives
Ideally you want to have "presence" with executives, being able to converse and be seen by executives both inside and outside your company as a colleague and a peer. Here are the Brilliant Practices to make this a reality:
- Earn the right to be there—do your homework. Use all the investigative approaches previously discussed in this book. Have an understanding of their business issues and personal wins down cold.

- Be ready to share something of value first before probing. An industry report, findings from a study, or just a relevant article can all work to position the conversation as important and establish you as a colleague.
- Think and act big-picture. Edit down 45 pages of a relevant study to three bullet points. Sort through a deck of slides for one overall diagram. Change your altitude from crop duster to fighter pilot.
- Link the conversation to how your capabilities and offerings will positively impact the executive's business issues and personal wins. Whether talking about systems integration, market research, or talent acquisition, connect your solution directly to revenue growth, market share, cost reduction, new market entry...whatever your research uncovered as the drivers important to that executive. Translate and net-out all technical issues into what executives care about—business performance. If what you have doesn't have a strong connection to what's important to the executive, don't have the conversation.
- Use your face cards when required. Sometimes executives prefer to talk to other executives. Bring along your executives when you think it will impact the persuasion process. However, guide and coach your executive on what to say, when, and how.
- An excellent way to start executive relationships is in a "non-business" setting. For example, if your company sponsors local executive forums, get into the audience and mingle.

Flash Point: Never meet with an executive without doing your homework and having something of probable interest to discuss. Otherwise, you will never be invited back.

Successful conversations don't just happen. Preparation, paired with practice, will help you help your customers (and everyone else) do the right things.

The next chapter will introduce a number of proven concepts that will allow you to practice all of the proactive ideas presented in this book. You will learn how to take charge of your time and your life for peak personal performance.

CHAPTER 8

Taking Charge of Your Time and Your Life for Peak Personal Performance

In this chapter, I introduce you to five brilliant time management practices to free up more of your time; help you set priorities that align with the highest value-adding, value-creating actions; and share ideas for making the work-life balance a reality for you. I will frame this within the context of your own personal blueprint for brilliance—think of it as a lighthouse, keeping you on the correct path to achieving what is most important to you in life, while avoiding becoming shipwrecked. The end result will be that you will generate better work, feel more in control, do more that is personally rewarding, and move your personal "fun meter" way over to the right.

Time Management Practice 1: Build Your Blueprint for Brilliance

As the saying goes, "If you are not sure where you want to go, any road will do." In other words, all this time management stuff can be a huge waste of time if you don't have a personal blueprint that charts out what you see as most important in life—and a course of action to achieve it. So, in actuality, this is not a time management practice, per se; it's more of a life management practice.

Before you begin creating tactical steps for time management, I highly recommend that you build your own strategic blueprint for brilliance, consisting of these components:

1. **Mission.** What is your mission, passion, and purpose in life?
2. **Principles.** What are your guiding principles—the values and truths that guide your thoughts and actions?
3. **Focus.** What is your focus? What are the most important things in your life (e.g., family, health, profession, personal growth, giving back)?
4. **Goals.** What are your goals that will help you achieve your mission in life?

Brilliantly Building Your Brand

As you plan out your path for progress, you will be including many aspects of self-development. This is another chance to use the powerful time management practice of the "double dip" introduced in Chapter 3. For example, if you will be reading one business book each quarter, volunteer to do four lunch-and-learns for your team, outlining the key concepts of each book and how they can be applied to improve team performance. This will demonstrate your prowess in a positive, relevant way. I'd also recommend that you volunteer to give presentations and submit articles for publication. Look for any and every opportunity to share your knowledge with others. Your skills will grow, your expertise will show, and you will be building your personal brand.

---

5. **Balance.** What steps will you take to achieve synergy and balance?
6. **Achievement.** How will you track, monitor, and adjust your actions to achieve your blueprint?

There are several excellent books on this topic that can help you build your blueprint for brilliance. I recommend *The Seven Habits of Highly Effective People,*[1] by Stephen Covey; *First Things First,*[2] by Stephen Covey, A. Roger Merrill, and Rebecca R. Merrill; as well as *How Will You Measure Your Life?,*[3] by Clayton Christensen, James Allworth, and Karen Dillon.

Study these books...invest the time...build your blueprint for brilliance...then move on to the next practice.

Time Management Practice 2: Practice What I Preach!

With your big-picture framework established via your personal blueprint for brilliance, it is time to get down to the nitty-gritty of taking control of your time.

Implementing Time Management Practice 2 is easy—put in place the Brilliant Practices you have learned in this book. Do this, and you will greatly increase your ability to do things right the first time, and thus save yourself and others the time and hassle of rework. In addition, when you apply the seven trust builders, demonstrate your customer acumen, listen with intensity, probe with purpose, present powerfully, and acknowledge concerns well, you create trust that leads to confidence in you and urgency to put your recommendations in place.

When you act like a BSP, you avoid the hemming and hawing, the discussing and kibitzing, the waiting and hoping. Problems are minimized or avoided altogether, the decision process is compressed, and much more time becomes available for you to proactively explore, with your willing customer, strategic solutions that lead to greater customer success. Late-night panic calls will be avoided, customers will readily agree to act based upon your schedule, and stress will be reduced all around.

> Flash Point: When you act like a brilliant service professional, you will sing the melody, the company will hum the harmony, and the customer will follow your tune.

Time Management Practice 3: Just Say No

The natural tendency of anyone brought up in the services industry is to say yes. Yes to helping a customer out with something "just a little" beyond scope. Yes to meeting marketing's seemingly endless requests for reference account examples. And yes to bailing a salesperson out who promised a ridiculous date on a customer go-live. In fact, yes is often the first word that comes out of a services professional's mouth.

In many situations, this is the right thing to do—suck it up for the good of the customer, your colleagues, and the company. A little extra effort on your part can do a lot of good. It is worth it.

Yet, there are some very negative aspects of saying yes too often. Based upon your agreeable past behavior, you set an unrealistic expectation with the people you deal with, as they assume you will always say yes to any requests. So when the customer or the salesperson or the marketer comes to you with a truly outrageous request and you refuse, he looks at you with disbelief and mutters phrases such as, "I wonder what has gotten into him!" Or, "She must be having a really bad day."

In addition, you are expending time on things that might have been much better spent elsewhere.

Furthermore (and of course it was not your intent), when you say yes a vast majority of the time, you establish a perception that you are a pushover. This will never be stated, but most cultures (especially Western ones) don't respect people who "don't stand up for themselves" or who "lack backbone." So your attempts at being a good team player backfire, and you are seen as being weak.

So what is the answer? If you've fallen into the "pattern of yes" described above, you can't just start saying no anytime you feel it's justified, or you'll get the reaction described earlier — it is too abrupt a change. You have to earn the right to say no.

You accomplish this by making a "just say no" personal strategy. Do your homework up front by defining appropriate boundaries of what you will do and what you will not do to make your

Playing Purposeful Politics

Like acne on a teenager, politics are always present and often annoying. Two-person fruit stands and small nonprofit organizations have politics just like huge companies and vast governments. My suggestion? Be totally aware that politics are going on all the time, but choose not to play. Speak negatively about no one. Do your job very well, think and act win-win-win, demonstrate the seven trust builders, and people will think highly of you — as one who is above gossiping. Some will not appreciate your nonparticipation, but better to be seen as a Goodie Two Shoes rather than a Brown-Nosing Suck-Up.

Finally, closely observe the behavior of members of the U.S. Congress, and never do anything that they do. Life is too short for the mean-spirited, self-serving politics of personal power.

customers, sales, and your services organization successful while supporting the overall business. Involve your management in the process to gain agreement on how to handle all of the special requests that you know from experience will occur, and get their commitment on how they will be handled. By involving others, and by having fair plans on what is acceptable and what is not, not only can you "do the right thing" for the business, but you can build and maintain your own personal credibility. The Brilliant Practice for saying no is this: Say yes when it counts, but just say no when it doesn't. Here is my suggested strategy:

Saying-No Scenarios
Illegal, Immoral, or Impossible
If you are certain the customer request is illegal, immoral, or impossible, you should say no at the time the request is made. To put off saying no immediately just wastes everyone's time. The five steps to saying no can be seen in Figure 8.1.

Inappropriate
The customer is not always right. If the customer requests something inappropriate (not in his best interest) and you know you will be supported by your management, say no at the time the request is made.

Flash Point: The customer is always right—baloney!

Out of Scope
If the customer requests something out of scope, and you have a scope-change plan in place, explain the impact of the change on the engagement, and then ask the customer to authorize the request.

If the customer has no scope-change plan in place or refuses to pay for the change in scope, say no at the time of the request if you are sure your management will support you. If the out-of-scope request is small, easy, and doesn't take much effort, it might take less time and less hassle than arguing with the customer. This may make the customer feel that "he owes you one" sometime in the future. Just like Marlon Brando used to say in the *Godfather* after doing a favor, "Someday you may be able to repay me with a small kindness." Or, maybe this customer has gotten the wrong end of the bull from your company. Use your discretion; just remember the possible drawbacks I mentioned earlier.

Management Support

I am sure you noticed that I recommend saying no for inappropriate and out-of-scope situations only if you know you'll have management support. If you know you'll have that support, then say no, ending this decision where it should be ended — with you. Sadly, however, I have often observed that if an important customer calls a senior manager in a company, often that manager will cave on the spot and give in to the customer, and your reputation has been significantly damaged. The customer now has your manager on speed dial and will call him at the least pushback you give to any request. You are out of the loop.

Brilliant Practice: If you have any doubts about management supporting you in telling the customer no, don't make the decision — tell the customer that you will pass it up to management to handle the situation as they see fit.

Figure 8.1

The Five Steps to Saying No

1. Acknowledge the customer's concern.
2. Provide an explanation.
3. Present alternatives.
4. Get the customer to buy in.
5. Thank the customer.

Here is a Shining Example that addresses how to handle an inappropriate situation using these steps:

Irritated Customer: "I keep telling you, I don't have the budget to buy the Maximo Converter!"

Brilliant Service Professional:

1. Acknowledge the customer's concern—remain calm, pause before responding, demonstrate empathy: "Suzanne, I get it. I understand budgets and having to live within them."
2. Provide an explanation: "However, I refuse to support a buying decision that isn't going to give you what you need. The Minimo Converter cannot deliver the precision required for your application. If you buy it, you will get nothing but rejects, hassle, and high blood pressure. I am pretty darn good, but I can't make chicken soup out of chicken feathers."
3. Present alternatives: "Maybe you would be best off waiting for your next budget cycle and trying to get additional funds. Another consideration, though you'd have to talk to our salespeople, could be a lease program. Can you think of any other options?"

    Customer: "What about a retrofit of our current equipment? I surely have budget for that."

    Brilliant Service Professional: "Good idea; that might work."
4. Get the customer to buy in: "I will put a team together to explore your suggestion and get back to you within a couple of days. OK?"
5. Thank the customer: "Thank you."

Here is a Shining Example that addresses how to handle an out-of-scope situation:

Smiling Customer: "Sammy, I don't know what I'd do without you. I'm going to tell that to your boss when I seem him next month at the Premier Customer Council. Oh, by the way, I'd really appreciate it if you would customize six more screens for me. I don't have any additional budget, but you are so fast, you could do it in no time."

Brilliant Service Professional:

1. Acknowledge the customer's concern—remain calm, pause before responding, demonstrate empathy: "Bill, I appreciate your comment, thank you. You know I enjoy working with you, and I appreciate the challenges of staying within budgets."

2. Provide an explanation: "However, I have to say no to your request. Tailoring those six screens would take at least six days of my time. It is not fair to my company to pass up the opportunity for billable hours helping other customers."

3. Present alternatives: "Possibly, those six screens can wait a few months until you get new funding? How about getting your marketing group to pay for it?"

   Customer: "Yeah, I can probably come up with the money somewhere."

4. Get the customer to buy in: "Great! Let me know when that happens, and we will get things scheduled."

5. Thank the customer: "Thanks for understanding."

Here's a Shining Example that responds to your boss's inappropriate request:

Your Boss: "Sammy, I need you to take the lead with Complexo right away. I need someone of your caliber to keep things from totally crashing."

Brilliant Service Professional:

1. Acknowledge the customer's (your boss's) concern—remain calm, pause before responding, demonstrate empathy: "Boss, I appreciate your confidence in me. I know how important Complexo is to the company."

2. Provide an explanation: "However, I need your help. You know I don't mind working hard, but right now I am totally slammed. There are not enough hours in the day for me to

take on Complexo, plus adequately deal with Orthogal. You know how temperamental they are."

Your Boss: "Yes, you are right."

3. Present alternatives: "Could you bring Franny back from Hong Kong to handle Complexo? Or how about you taking care of Orthogal for a few months?"

4. Get your boss to buy in: "I want you to take Complexo. I'll find someone else to take on Orthogal by Friday."

5. Thank your boss: "Thanks, Boss."

Savvy readers will quickly see that in this scenario, the Saying No model is a negotiation tool, and is very powerful in dealing with demanding bosses!

Time Management Practice 4: Corral the Nags and Ride Your Horses

We all know that different people have different personalities that shape their philosophy of life and drive their day-to-day behavior. For example, you may know individuals who in their personal lives treat every customer service conversation as a debate, view sales clerks as lackeys to do their bidding, and often demand that waitresses send back their main course on some minor issue, and then refuse to pay for the meal and leave no tip. Conversely, caring people, like us, treat people with respect, appreciate their expertise, and will gladly pay for the extra value they bring.

Your customer organizations have personalities also. Some customer organizations assume an arrogance usually reserved for politicians and prima donnas. They view you as a Replaceable Vendor, believing that you, your organization, and your offerings are like a swappable part on a lawnmower, an easily interchangeable commodity. They only want to see you when they want something—and when they do, they expect it immediately. If you don't give them what they ask for, when they ask for it, they yell, scream, and threaten to drop your company as a supplier if you don't comply. They will suck up all your efforts like a Hoover vacuum cleaner extracting cat hair off a sofa, and they always expect that everything you give them should be free because they are so big and so important.

Your sales guys and execs call them key accounts and coddle them like English royalty because they buy large volumes of products. However, if your company ever added up the cost of the deep discounts and freebies they gave away to these leeches and plugged it into the profitability calculation, they would discover that they are probably losing money on them. I call these customers Nags. Alas, having to deal with at least a few of these accounts is pretty much a rodeo reality to the service pro.

Luckily, other customers value your capabilities and respect you and your organization—they see you and your company as a Valuable Supplier. After you have established your competence and built professional trust, they will openly talk to you about their challenges and opportunities and gladly hear your recommendations to improve their performance. Most important, they will pay for the value you create. These customers are your Workhorses—treat them well and they will respond in kind, with mutual gain for both parties.

If you are fortunate, you may have the opportunity to work with a customer that sees your company as a Vital Partner. They will gladly pay for the value you provide, as they are constantly trying to capture unique insights or capabilities that they can use to build strategic business advantage. These customers will constantly challenge you and your organization to take things to the next level. These customers are your Thoroughbreds. Nurturing these relationships takes lots of TLC, but the potential rewards are great.

Figure 8.2 outlines my suggestion that you match the effort

you expend on each customer personality type based upon their supplier philosophy. Since your Workhorses and Thoroughbreds have much more potential value than your Nags, it makes good horse sense for you to expend more time and effort on them.

Figure 8.2

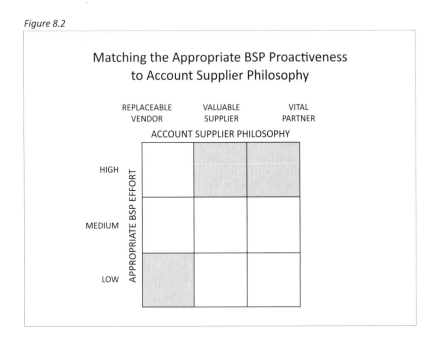

Matching the Appropriate BSP Proactiveness to Account Supplier Philosophy

Delivering on the Customer Promise

Let me be clear: You and your company have an obligation to deliver on the customer promise for all of your accounts. However, I recommend that you think and act differently to get the job done, depending on the customer personality. Here is my suggested process:

1. Place each of your customers into one of the three categories just described: Nags, Workhorses, and Thoroughbreds. This is not difficult to do. After having any contact with them at all, you will quickly learn their philosophy toward you and your company.

2. Accept the reality. Don't be too disheartened if many of the

accounts you service see you as a Replaceable Vendor — that is just the reality. Now some of you may be thinking that if you work hard enough and long enough, you can change the perception of these Nags to see you and your company as a Valuable Supplier and pay for the value you add to their business. My response is straightforward: "When pigs fly!"

Hoping for this transformation is exactly like trying to change the personality of Uncle Max. (Doesn't everyone have an Uncle Max?) Uncle Max tells bad, politically incorrect jokes over family holiday get-togethers. He chews, talks, and dribbles simultaneously at the dinner table. And he always wears his stained pants too low, like a plumber fixing a kitchen drain. Yet, no matter how much Aunt Patty tries to persuade, coerce, threaten, or plead with him, Uncle Max will not change. Uncle Max is Uncle Max and will stay Uncle Max unless something very dramatic and very rare occurs. Companies are the same way. So accept your Nags for what they are — efforts to change them are almost always futile.

3. Embrace the appropriate strategy for each of the three customer types:

- **Nags.** For the Nags who see you as a Replaceable Vendor, stop pampering a horse that won't run! Give them the bare minimum that meets the service level agreement that you have with them, and no more. Be driven by efficiency. Don't communicate face-to-face if you can do it by phone. Better yet, don't call, use e-mail. Even better yet, get them to self-service themselves via your website. And say no to requests that are out of scope. Don't try to be proactive, because they will not appreciate it or pay for it. Unless the Nag customer is screaming at your boss that you are not doing enough, you are doing too much. Applying this strategy will not only save you time, but it also will save you grief and give you the same sense of calm that some people achieve through yoga or meditation.

- **Workhorses.** The Workhorses, the customers that see you as a Valuable Supplier, are your sweet spot. The strategy for them is effectiveness. Take every minute of time you have wasted with the Nags to saddle up your Workhorses. With these accounts, try to delegate, persuade, or coerce others in your services organization to handle the reactive part of the job while you focus on being proactive by strategically working on making the customer more successful. If you act like a BSP, they will value what you do and pay for what you do. They will forge a strong alliance with you, purchase more from you each year, and become a client for life.

Dousing the Flames of Customers from Hell

Most customers are good people who listen to reason and act fairly. Occasionally, however, you run across a customer who is obnoxious, manipulative, or just plain mean. They seem to take sadistic pleasure in making simple things complex and blaming others for their own shortcomings. Customers from Hell are phenomenally adept at one thing: making everyone around them miserable. If you get stuck with one of these customers, I suggest these strategies:

1. Fire them. If possible, sever the relationship and never see or talk to them again. Ideally, use your powers of persuasion to help them become customers of your biggest competitor. This is the ideal scenario, as the more pain your competitors receive, the more gain you can achieve.
2. Get them assigned to someone else in your organi-

- **Thoroughbreds.** If you have one of those rare customers that is looking for Vital Partners, you and your organization have a sweet dilemma. On one hand, the opportunities are huge. On the other hand, a customer like this can tie up vast amounts of your organization's resources for long periods of time. Working closely with them will have a strategic impact on your company that is hopefully good, but possibly could be bad if your company's vision and mission are not synergistic with theirs. The strategy for Vital Partners is a focus on innovation. I suggest you involve your boss and your leadership team to discuss the most appropriate role—for you and for your organization.

zation. This is quite selfish, but if you are a BSP, you have some clout in your company, and this is a great time to use it.

3. If strategies 1 and 2 are not options, do your best to avoid these customers. Follow the same approach outlined above in dealing with Nags. Remember, you will not change them. Make it a game: Don't be upset and have no regret; smile all the while.

   a. Take no abuse. If customers scream, swear, or abuse you in any way, calmly and professionally leave the premises or depart the phone call. Life is too short to deal with jerks.

   b. Document everything. Sadly, exiting a bad relationship is often troubling. Your management and HR will probably be involved. Hence, it is prudent to document every contact and every situation.

Time Management Practice 5: Do the Focus Hocus Pocus

Focusing is one of the most powerful ways to control your time and thus control your life. The four practices introduced above are all about focus. This time management practice introduces a handy tool to hone this focus even further. I call it the Focus Hocus Pocus because if you follow these guidelines, your time management capabilities will seem magical.

The Time Management Grid
The tool to use to help you gain control of your time is the Time Management Grid, seen in Figure 8.3. It is recognized as the standard mechanism for helping you understand where your time is spent today and ideally where you should prioritize and spend time tomorrow. I like it and recommend it because it is simple and easy to use. The Time Management Grid identifies time usage based upon the perceived importance and urgency of the activity. Let's review the four quadrants of the grid, one at a time.

Figure 8.3

Time Management Grid

Important and Urgent	Important but Not Urgent
Reality: Necessity	Reality: Leadership
Not Important but Presumed Urgent	Not Important and Not Urgent
Reality: Deception	Reality: Waste

Not Important and Not Urgent
Inside this quadrant are the things you do that are not important and not urgent to achieving your goals. Since by definition they are not important, they don't add any value. Boredom, procrastination, or fear may lead you to partake in activities that fall into this category, such as playing *Angry Birds*, reading English romance novels, or watching videos of cute dogs on YouTube. Yes, there is some value in diversion or escape occasionally, but for the most part, items in this category are a waste of time.

Not Important but Presumed Urgent
These are the things that may appear urgent and/or important, but are not. Often many activities fall into this category, e.g., reading and responding to most e-mails and phone calls, reading or writing some reports, most all spontaneous chit-chat, and attending numerous meetings.

For example, I have seen countless customer meetings organized by the sales team where they ask a technical person (sometimes several) to attend "just in case" the customer asks a question, such as, "What is the potential impact to your product viscosity if sea levels rise dramatically in the Arctic in August?" The truth is that items in this category create a deception that drives efforts far beyond the speed and scope of response necessary.

Important and Urgent
As a service professional, most of the things you do fall into the Important and Urgent category. These activities are the core requirements of your job. Examples of Important and Urgent activities may include reacting to a crisis, such as down hardware or faulty software, responding to customer questions, completing projects on tight deadlines, or following up on executive requests that need a real-time response. These are all things requiring immediate attention. Items in this quadrant are a necessity,

and obviously become a priority when the red "do it now" button has been pushed.

Important but Not Urgent

Items in the Important but Not Urgent quadrant are strategic actions that can add long-term value but don't have a pending deadline. Internal examples might include improving processes to enhance quality or simplifying procedures so that specific tasks take less time to perform. External examples might include proactively investing time in building relationships that generate trust and lead to the discovery of new opportunities.

Personal critical actions in this category are those that impact your personal leadership. Increasing your customer acumen or expanding your soft-skills prowess is vital to your long-term success, but these activities rarely come with a deadline. Getting adequate sleep and exercise, and spending quality time with your family, inhabit this quadrant as well.

Important but Not Urgent activities are often very easy to put off for days, weeks, months, or even years. Whenever you hear someone say, "Someday I'll..." ("...take my spouse to Hawaii, learn French, study philosophy, take a course in management...") you are probably hearing something important to that person, but not urgent enough for them to take action. You may have longtime friends who for years have repeated this "Someday I'll..." mantra; sadly, you know their "someday" will never happen.

The reality is that items in this quadrant determine your future success.

Get the Data

The starting point of benefitting from the Time Management Grid is getting good data on where you are now. To determine this baseline, log your time for a couple of weeks and analyze where your time really goes. Place each activity into one of the four quadrants. Use this information to establish the percentage of time you spend in each of the four categories. Next, set objectives to change those ratios to those more in line with what you want out of life.

Turning the Fodder of the Time Management Grid into the Fuel for Your Time Machine

Now it is time to implement strategies to revamp your focus and accomplish your objectives.

Figure 8.4 shows the recommended strategies for each of the four quadrants. Adopting and implementing these strategies will fuel your own time machine and help you accomplish the important things in your life, easier and faster.

Figure 8.4

Time Management Strategies

Important and Urgent	Important but Not Urgent
Strategy: Reduce	Strategy: Increase
Not Important but Presumed Urgent	Not Important and Not Urgent
Strategy: Minimize	Strategy: Avoid

The suggested strategy for Not Important and Not Urgent activities is pretty straightforward: Avoid them.

- **Stop—cold turkey.** Immediately stop doing anything not important and not urgent.
- **Substitute.** If you feel the need to do something "off task," substitute a Not Important and Not Urgent activity with an

Important but Not Urgent one. Read Peter Drucker instead of Jane Austen. Watch TED presentations instead of YouTube bloopers.

- **Reward.** If you are addicted to *Angry Birds* (such as a projected 20 million people are) and can't give it up, save it as a reward. When you accomplish an Important but Not Urgent task, make playing *Angry Birds* a 15-minute treat—you deserve it.

The recommended strategy for Not Important but Presumed Urgent activities is to minimize them.

- **Use non-peak time.** Schedule your non-peak time for these less-important things that aren't really urgent that you still have to do, such as responding to most e-mails, completing expense reports, or answering a marketing survey, and clump them into groups so that you do them all at one time. For me, that is late afternoon when I have gotten the real work done.
- **Touch an item only once.** Don't skim or file Not Important tasks; touch them once and be done with them.
- **Question.** Question the owner of every meeting you are requested to attend. Ask the following: Why is it vital that I attend? What is my role? Is there someone else who is adequately qualified to substitute for me? Would a one-page summary on the topic suffice?
- **Double-dip.** For example, if you feel you must attend a low-value teleconference call, put yourself on mute and handle those e-mails, expense reports, or customer updates.
- **Don't do it.** Don't do some of the things presumed urgent and see what happens. Often no one will notice. If it is important, they will get back to you.

The suggested strategy for Important and Urgent activities is to make every effort to reduce them. Customer lines will go down, software sometimes has a mind of its own, and customers will want, ask, or demand immediate service. That will not change, and when it occurs you need to react.

- **Challenge urgency.** Oftentimes, anything the customer is not happy about, they perceive as urgent — and they communicate it that way to you. But as we all know, not all issues demand that you drop everything and board the bus to Boise. Urgency must be challenged. When the customer pushes the alarm, it is your job to scope out the intensity of the fire: How big is it? Where is it? What is the possible/probable impact? Is it really a fire or just something smoldering? Using the four relationship skills to professionally and respectfully challenge each issue is a powerful tool in prioritizing the actions of both you and your team.
- **Predict.** Talk with your customers and proactively predict some of the things that might go wrong, and probably will go wrong, with your products, and then collaborate to decide how to deal with each one when it happens.
- **Identify.** Identify the most common and the most time-consuming issues. Individually and as a team apply quality techniques to identify root causes and find better ways of doing things.
- **Delegate when you can.** Anytime there is the opportunity to pass on reactive work to someone else on your team, consider it.
- **Negotiate less-important requests.** As you saw earlier in the section on saying no, when your plate is full but your boss wants more, involve him in the prioritization process. Ask him what he wants you to do (and, hence, not do). Use your persuasion skills to keep you on your most important tasks and avoid less-important requests.

The recommended strategy for Important but Not Urgent activities is, by all means, increase them.

- **Use your saved time wisely.** The time saved from applying the three strategies above could easily amount to an additional two hours or more each day. Funnel that saved time into this quadrant with gusto.

- **Less is more.** One of the driving principles of quality giant Joseph Juran was understanding and applying the concept of the useful many versus the critical few. The useful many are all potential value adders, but the critical few are the probable value creators—the big rocks compared to the smaller pebbles that can have by far the most impact on your work performance and personal success. For example, it is much easier to get your arms around a small number of critical key performance indicators than it is to address a dozen objectives. Ideally, focus on no more than three issues.
- **Target.** To accomplish the outcomes you desire in your blueprint for brilliance, your personal plan should heavily reflect your Important but Not Urgent activities. I suggest you plan on a yearly, quarterly, monthly, and weekly basis to accomplish, monitor, and adjust those objectives.
- **Use a to-do list.** A to-do list helps you target your focus. Keeping in mind all the Important and Urgent activities that seem to pop up, be realistic in what you try to accomplish.
- **Schedule.** Schedule Important but Not Urgent work at your peak times. For most of us, that is first thing in the morning. Also, schedule exercise and sleep, as you are not much use to anyone if you are exhausted or ill.
- **Balance work and life.** It is so easy to focus on work now and think, *Someday I'll...*, when it comes to your personal life. Unless you take aggressive measures, your personal life will take second place. So schedule time with your friends and family, including dates with your spouse, and then honor those commitments. For example, if your job requires travel, once a quarter take your spouse or family along, especially if it is someplace fun or exciting. If business takes you to Las

Vegas (and your spouse likes Vegas), tack on a couple extra days to just hang together.

Flash Point: When you pit a to-do list against a schedule, the schedule wins every time.

Once you rearrange your priorities around your life goals, good things happen. Your work-life balance becomes harmonious, time for the most important things emerge, stress goes down, and fun goes up. Take charge of your life and time, and pave your path to peak personal performance.

Last Words

There you have it—my best thinking on what it takes to be the value-creating, rock-star-in-the-spotlight, brilliant service professional.

Hats off to all of you who embrace this life-changing opportunity and commit to personal brilliance. If you want it, you can achieve it.

I'll see you on the center stage.

References and Notes

Introduction

1. I talk in detail about the rising criticality of services within product companies and the opportunities and challenges it brings in my book *Seriously Selling Services: How to Build a Profitable Services Business in Any Industry*.
2. Alexander, James A. 2007. "Transitioning Technical Experts into Trusted Advisors." St. James City, FL: Alexander Consulting.

Chapter 1

1. Adapted from *Clients for Life: How Great Professionals Develop Breakthrough Relationships*, by Jagdish Sheth and Andrew Sobel. 2000. New York: Simon & Schuster.

Chapter 2

1. Maister, David, Charles H. Green, and Robert M. Galford. 2001. *The Trusted Advisor*. New York: Touchstone.
2. Rent the movie *Tin Men* with Danny DeVito for an excellent and funny example of salespeople at their worst.
3. Cialdini, Robert B. 2006. *Influence: The Psychology of Persuasion*. New York: HarperBusiness.
4. Gunnery, Sarah D. 2013."The deliberate Duchenne smile: perceptions and social outcomes." Psychology Dissertations. Paper 31. http://hdl.handle.net/2047/d20003145.
5. Source: The Likeability Factor. http://www.amazon.com/The-Likeability-Factor-L-Factor-Achieve/dp/1400080509.
6. Ibid.
7. Borrowed from Leonard L. Berry, one of the best researchers and writers regarding service.

Chapter 3

1. Donofrio, Nicholas, Jim Spohrer, and Hossein S. Zadeh. September 7, 2009. "Research-Driven Medical Education and Practice: A Case for T-Shaped Professionals." MJA. http://www.ceri.msu.edu/wp-content/uploads/2010/06/A-Case-for-T-Shaped-Professionals-20090907-Hossein.pdf.
2. In the classes I teach, I provide my students with a recommended reading and listening list for building customer acumen and other life skills. I'll be happy to send you a complimentary copy. Just email me at alex@alexanderstrategists.com.
3. Drucker, Peter F. 1993. *Management: Tasks, Responsibilities, Practices*. New York: HarperBusiness.

Chapter 4

1. "Sales Behavior Observation Research." 1984. Xerox Learning Systems.
2. Carnegie, Dale. 1998. *How to Win Friends and Influence People*. New York: Pocket Books. (Dale Carnegie does a great job of providing the rationale and examples of this important skill along with other great tips in this book. I highly, highly recommend this classic.)

Chapter 6

1. Pink, Daniel. 2012. *To Sell Is Human: The Surprising Truth About Moving Others*. New York: Riverhead.
2. Alexander, James A., 2004. "Everybody Sells Services." *The Professional Journal*. Fort Myers: AFSMI.
3. Alexander, James A. 2009. *Seriously Selling Services: How to Build a Profitable Services Business in Any Industry*. Fort Myers: Alexander Consulting. p44.
4. Alexander, James A. 2007. *Transitioning Technical Experts into Trusted Advisors*. Fort Myers: Alexander Consulting.
5. Koch, Chris. 2011. "ITSMA's Eight Big B2B Marketing Trends for 2011." http://www.itsma.com/ezine/eight-b2b-marketing-trends-for-2011/.

Chapter 8

1. Covey, Stephen R. 2004. *The Seven Habits of Highly Effective People*. New York: Free Press.
2. Covey, Stephen R., A. Roger Merrill, and Rebecca R. Merrill. 1996. *First Things First*. New York: Free Press.
3. Christensen, Clayton M., James Allworth, and Karen Dillon. 2012. *How Will You Measure Your Life?* New York: Harper Business.

Index

About the Author

James "Alex" Alexander, Ed.D, helps product companies build brilliant services businesses. He re-searches, publishes, advises, trains, and speaks on transforming good services organizations into high-performance services machines that create loyal customers, drive sales of  services and products, and dominate the competition. Contact Alex at alex@alexanderstrategists.com.